The Dalesman Bedside Book

compiled by
David Joy

DALESMAN

First Published in Great Britain 1993 by
Dalesman Publishing Company Limited,
Stable Courtyard, Broughton Hall,
Skipton, North Yorkshire BD23 3AE
Text © 1993 **Dalesman Publishing Company Ltd.**

Front cover by Ionicus.

British Library Cataloguing-in-Publication Data.
A catalogue record for this book is available from the British Library

ISBN **1 85568 065 3**
Typeset by **Lands Services**
Printed by **Biddles Limited**

CONTENTS

FOREWORD

Since its first appearance in April 1939, the *Dalesman* has published well over 15 million words on Yorkshire and its people. Delving through past volumes in the preparation of this anthology has been a long but rewarding journey. It has confirmed that one of the magazine's great virtues is that each and every copy still retains its freshness, ten, twenty or more years after publication. It has also revealed the immense riches that lie waiting to be re-discovered in the earlier issues. For here are inspiring words by such well-known Yorkshire authors as Phyllis Bentley, Arthur Raistrick, Ella Pontefract, William Riley and Dorothy Una Ratcliffe.

The *Dalesman Bedside Book* is primarily a personal selection of articles not too long and not too short that I feel have stood the test of time or have extra-special appeal. I hope these pages both inform and entertain, and reflect the spirit of Yorkshire in all its glorious and infinite variety.

David Joy
Editor, Dalesman
1988–1993

1
YORKSHIRE FOLK

YORKSHIRE CHARACTER

OUR bleak northern climate, our northern hills, perhaps the drop of Danish blood in our heredity, the independent economic structure of the early textile trade, our distance through many centuries from the centre of the country's culture, perhaps even William the Conqueror's fire and sword – some of these factors at any rate – have combined to produce in Yorkshire a character which is admitted by all who know it to be unyielding though sincere; conscious of its own skill and proud of it, and not at all disposed to modify its idiosyncrasies for the sake of other people. In a word: a character sturdy, warm-hearted, independent, but somewhat stubborn and reserved.

Reserved? Yes, I think that reserve, the dislike of excessive expression, is one of the most significant ingredients in the Yorkshire character. My two favourite stories about Yorkshire folk both illustrate this trait. Here is the first of them.

I was walking along a Pennine hill outside Halifax one glorious spring day. The sky was blue with white clouds driving swiftly across to the horizon, the sun shone and the many hills rolling away into the distance were clearly visible, green close at hand, blue far away. Passing an old man mending a dry-stone wall, I nodded to him and said mildly: "Fine day!" He straightened up, gave me a look of intense contempt and remarked: "Nay, don't let's get into a lather about it!"

My other story concerns a young couple who courted for several years without the young man ever coming to the point of matrimony. They strolled about of an evening in silence. At last one night the young man said abruptly: "Mary, wilt 'a wed me?" "I will," said Mary. Nothing more was said. They continued to stroll in silence, until at last they reached the door of Mary's home. Mary, wishing to clinch the matter,

enquired: "Hasn'ta owt else to say to me, lad?" "Ah've said too
much already," was his reply.

Phyllis Bentley (1958)

THE MEANEST MAN

I F it is an old Yorkshire custom to be "tight wi' thi brass"
it is only because economic necessity has decreed caution
in matters of finance. One cannot deny that there are
mean people in Yorkshire, as elsewhere, and it was a Topcliffe
character who earned himself the title of "Meanest Man in
Yorkshire". He was "Old John Mealy-Face", and he was born
in 1784.

John obtained his queer nickname in the following manner.
Knowing the wasteful habits of women, he refused to allow
his wife to bake bread while he was out in case she cut off a
piece and ate it before he could get back. But one day, while
he was at Thirsk market, she did bake a loaf and ate almost
the whole of it.

Old John found out and was very wrath. To stop her doing it
again, he used to press his face down into the flour at the top
of the bin before going to market, and on his return would put
his face back into the impression so as to be quite sure that
the flour had not been disturbed in his absence.

There is a modern comparison in the story, which I believe
is true, of a man in a West Riding town. A workmate met him
as he was on his way to the mill. "Tha saands ter 'ev a lot
o' brass," said the friend as they walked along. "Brass be
blowed," was the reply, "it's mi wife's false teeth. There's too
much being 'etten at ahr 'ouse between meals."

F. Sparling (1959)

THE ROAD TO DESTRUCTION

E RIC Treacy, Bishop of Wakefield, has had much to say
about Yorkshire, describing the county as a kingdom
in miniature, with five universities, five cathedrals,

five cities, mountains, moors, potholes, slag heaps, smoke and fumes and a lot of catarrh, and the Yorkshireman as suspicious, obstinate, materialist, isolationist, non-conformist, and blunt – "and I like him as he is."

Although conscious of having lived in Yorkshire for only 23 years, he is firmly in favour of its people. He once wrote of Halifax folk: "To hear them talk you would think that they were blunt, close-fisted, difficult to know, and hostile to strangers. Nothing could be further from the truth. They are wonderfully ready with praise and appreciation, generous when they are convinced that a cause is worthy of support, hospitable to strangers."

Dr. Treacy feels England is split into two halves, the North and the South. "The southerner thinks of the northerner as an uncultured ruffian, thriving on brass bands, breeding whippets, eating fish and chips, drinking oceans of beer, and playing a particularly savage form of Rugby football. Northern misconceptions of the South are that they are all la-de-dah, snobbish and pretentious, slick and not be to trusted and living on the sweat and toil of the North."

He recently developed this theme in a call for northerners, and particularly West Riding folk, to stop being so conceited. Their belief that they were superior to people living south of the Trent was creating narrow parochialism, stubbornness, inflexibility and hence a lack of ideas. It was the road to destruction.

David Joy (1968)

AUNTIE LIL

"**H**AVE this child christened immediately," said the doctor. "She won't see another day." So they named her Lilian – and she has lived to see well over sixty years!
Her father was a mill-worker, but work was scarce and there was no unemployment pay in those "good old days". When out of work he eked out a meagre living with a hand-loom in the garret, sending the children out with the finished goods so that they might get a copper for taking it.

Lil grew up in a family where hard work was the order of

the day and their fun had to be home-made. She was no model child and was often to be found fishing in Yeadon Dam instead of being at school. Once, so 'tis said, she rode home on the "hoss-muck" cart in her best white party frock.

Very early in her housewifely career she was given the regular job of cleaning the knives and forks. Now Lil didn't like cleaning knives and forks but she *did* like telling stories, so her two younger brothers cleaned the cutlery whilst she improved their knowledge of "Cinderella" or "Jack the Giant Killer".

At twelve or so the children started in the mill as half-timers, graduating to full time within a year or two. Lil and her eldest sister also had to help in the home and with the younger children, for Lil's mother had a faulty heart.

One day it fell to Lil's lot to make her first Yorkshire pudding for their family of eight. After more than an hour in the oven the pudding was discovered boiling merrily. On being asked how much flour she had put in the mixture, Lil replied, "Just a bit in t'bottom o' t'basin."

Then there was the laundry class. "Bring something to iron next week," said the instructor, and everyone duly turned up with the usual small article – except Lil. *She* appeared carrying a clothes basket full to the brim with a week's ironing for eight!

Her mother died in 1916, and in the same year her "young man" was killed on the Somme. Lil did not feel able to face up to life any more until one day, on a tram, a man from a military hospital, minus arms and legs was carried on and jovially entertained the passengers. His courage did something to Lil and she took heart again.

The rest of her story is mainly one of keeping house for her father and maintaining her job in the mill as a weaver. She was even yet no expert at housekeeping, for there are still the tales of the tea-cakes she made which killed the pigs, of how she served her brother's friend with a marble in his stew on his first visit and of what she did with the hash for two when ten turned up for supper.

But Lil, with all her failings, had one great gift – a kind and loving heart. Everywhere she went she made friends, perhaps because she always took such pains to understand the other person's point of view, always ready to help where help was needed, always ready to give her last penny to someone she thought more needy.

She loved children and, having none of her own, she became universal auntie and "playmate" to those of other people. Sometimes at Christmas she would take a crowd of them to see a pantomime or Father Christmas, one tram-conductor on such an excursion being heard to remark, "Are these all yours, missus?"

I. Greaves (1952)

THE OLD ORDER CHANGETH

W E have lived to see a new order of folk peopling our Yorkshire dales. Still delightful they may be, even still racy of the soil and apparently fitting into their surroundings. The surroundings are the same, the everlasting hills remain but the *genus homo* is no longer the rough hewn, independent, distinct type we knew only a few decades ago.

There are buses running through the dales, there is a constant influx of visitors. A railway journey is now no longer feared, the big towns are no longer both inaccessible and full of danger and risks. The barriers have been broken, by wireless and other channels news of the outside world pours into what were the most isolated districts and roads have been so improved the steam thresher can travel to hill-side farms, hence the flail has been ousted. Dales women have tired of peat and the open fireplaces, and coals (delivered by motor-lorries) now burn in new-fashioned grates. Witchcraft, spells and the evil-eye are laughed at.

Many children attend schools in the distant town, the dialect has given place to B.B.C. English (except when a few old folk get together over their mugs of ale at the dale pub). Young men have wooed and won maidens from afar and infused new blood and new ideas into the dales, and everywhere, that which so charmed many of us in our youth is giving place to modern ideas, modern conceptions, modern meretriciousness and tinsel.

The mentality of a people has been debauched in a generation. They may be broader minded, more communicative, better informed, and possessed of greater self-confidence, they may be less marked as belonging to the hill-sides and heath lands, and they may feel that they are more abreast of the times than their conservative come-day-go-day, God send Sunday, forebears. But what has been the price? – the sacrifice of character, the selling of a birthright, for a mess of pottage which is to make us all as alike as peas in a pod with the shallow townsman as our model.

The result does not justify the price. I for one am glad to have known the true type of Yorkshire dales folk – the true, natural, unpretentious, blunt, men and women of the hill-sides and little valleys.

J. Fairfax-Blakeborough (1939)

2
AS IT IS SPOKE

THE LIVING SPEECH
OF YORKSHIRE

I ONCE heard an old man, sitting, leaning on his stick, in a rattling hill-going West Riding tram, shouting above the din into his neighbour's ear, "Aye, aw know yond; aw've never spokken to him, but aw can tell thi what he is, cos aw saw what he laughed at."

I had not seen what he laughed at. I had not seen him at all. But I knew what Old Moses meant, because I, too, am Yorkshire, and because out here, on the hillsides and the hill tops, laughter is of the heart and mind, and the heart and mind are of the wind and the rain and the cold sunshine – the keen biting wind, driving and hard and sometimes cruel, but the *cruelty* of any of it is the cruelty of the forces, determined and inexorable, never crafty, seldom man made.

We hear much of this talk about talk, the language of the people, and how it came and whence it came and I suppose that, delving among the languages in their making, there is much to be found that might be put together like a jig-saw puzzle, fitting here and there, coinciding now and then, but with many gaps and many contradictions which it is not easy to fit in.

There are long roads in the Riding, leading out, getting harder and higher as they go, narrowing and climbing, meeting the wind and the rain, crouching under the cold mist, with boggy places and long reaches where the path can hide itself, and the boulders are black and chining, but where at times the sun will come and a great warmth embrace it all and show it golden and green and grey with glinting water. All these things have taken shape in the words of the people and in the character of the people of which their words are the mirror.

Out of these has their independence been made, the spirit that wants nowt for nowt, that cannot be beholden and that knows such a growing fear of being beholden that the saving spirit hides the bank book and hides the smile, and even hides the kindness while the heart is full of it.

The words of this rough-hewn speech they say are dying out, but I cannot think they can ever pass away while there are fells and moors fostering their bitter sweetness, while there are mills where the looms weave much more than carpets and cloth, where great hopes and loves and fears travel with the shuttle. As long as these things are we shall be of them, making them part of us, and putting them into our words and our silences, as the moor bird and the sheep, whose call is the voice of the great spaces and their own loneliness.

Eleanor Gaukroger (1940)

CRICKETING TALES

C RICKET, more than any other sport or game, is productive of a never-ending galaxy of yarns and anecdotes. There are many reasons for this: its slower tempo, giving time for humour and repartee; its age-range of participants, its umpires (especially volunteers), and its knowledgeable spectators, who combine loyalty with the appreciative.

Willie Watson tells of a visiting player at Bramall Lane. He had a white scarf as a cravat, and constantly fiddled with it. Twice he let the ball go through to the boundary. He gave the scarf a tug. Then he missed a catch. A voice yelled, "Tha wants to pull that damned thing really TIGHT."

Vic Wilson took his benefit in 1958 at Sheffield. He was batting when it was announced that a collection taken for him the previous day had raised £268. He raised his cap high in grateful acknowledgment, and a "wag" in the crowd cried: "'E hasn't got enough. 'E's going round with 'is 'at now."

From I.A.R. Peebles comes the story of a day of murk and rain when Leicester visited Bramall Lane. The Yorks. captain and C.H. Taylor (skipper of Leicester) made frequent inspections of the wicket. At tea-time came the final inquest, and the former signalled regretfully to the few spectators that there was no hope – no play today. At that a window overlooking the ground was thrown up, and a voice hoarse with frustration bawled: "Dost tha think that Ah pays rent to stay in Bramall Lane for this?"

Leeds can claim for Headingley that Sheffield has not a monopoly of pungent comment. A.A. Thomson watched a game there when a weak opposing side (was it Leicester?) was tumbled out a second time early on the afternoon of the second day. "Hey," yelled his temporary neighbour, "take Verity off; we've paid a shilling."

That delightful writer of earlier times, "A Country Vicar", whose boyhood was spent at Braithwell near Rotherham, wrote in *The Happy Cricketer* of a Roses battle at Leeds. Said a Yorkshire spectator to a Lancashire neighbour: "We play nobbut 'ome-born men; ye'll play owt."

Lancastrian: "Wor Lord 'Awke born i' Yorkshire?"

Yorkist: "Well, that were nobbut a sort of accident like, tha knows." There followed a confused account of mischance of birth.

Lancastrian: "I tell thee, Lord 'Awke's no Yorkshireman. 'E's an importation, same as ours."

Yorkist (speechless for a while, then slowly and deliberately): "If a cat 'as kittens in a fried-fish shop, does that mek 'em kippers?"

J.E. Perry (1965)

THER'S NIVVER NOWT BUT WHAT THER'S SUMMAT

Ther's nivver nowt but what ther's summat;
So mi muther offen used to say.
They wer words I heeard not once or twice,
But monny a time ivvery day.

One Mundy when shoo's getten t'weshin aht,
An' t' bright sun had given place to rain,
Shoo looked disgusted at the darkened sky
And uttered her lugubrious refrain.

When in t' midst o' cleaning dahn in Spring,
T'hahse looked like t'owd chapel's jummle sale,
Who but parson should pop his horns in,
An' evoke the saying without fail.

Aye, that were mi muther's fav'rit speyk,
As much as t'word "welcome" on t'doormat,
An' with her dying breath at last, shoo said:
Ther's nivver nowt but what ther's summat.
                                    William T. Burkitt (1964)

NATIVE HUMOUR

BROAD Yorkshire sometimes contains the philosophy of the Yorkshireman, a homely philosophy often crystallised into his proverbial sayings: "Daftness niver built owt worth leavin' up"; "Niver judge t'blade byd heft"; "Sweetness of a posy mainly hings on wheer it comes fra"; "You can't graft on a botthery!" (said, for the comfort of schoolmasters, of a pupil who could not learn). "It's a good hoss 'at niver stummles, an' a good wife 'at niver grummles." "Them 'at niver diz nowt theirsens allus thinks 'at ther's nowt i'd wolld 'at's hard ti dea!"

It illustrates the Yorkshireman's wit and humour too, a many-sided homour, genuine, unforced, the humour of everyday things; frosty sometimes, like the folk who speak our tongue, hitting shrewdly and sometimes hard, but with nothing bitter or rankling about it. For example, I have heard in conversation, "He's a bit ower young, mebbe?" "Aye, why, that's a ailment 'at cures itsen wi'oot callin' t'doctor in!" Or again, "Ah sh'd ha' thowt he wad ha' had mair sense!" "Why, he hes all t'sense he was born wi' – he's niver used ony!"

Where else but in Yorkshire could you find an umpire who in one innings could give these decisions: "How is it?" "Not oot, but thoo will be if thoo diz it agean!" Later, "How's that?" "OOT!" "Oot? What for?" "For t'rest o'd day!" And still later. "How is it?" "Oot!" "Ah wasn't oot!" "Wasn't tha! Thoo just luke i'd Malton Gazette o' Settherday, an' thoo'll see whether thoo was oot or not!"

Two farmers met in the Pickering market-place. One said, "Hoo diz tha like ma new suit? Ah've had it made to measure." The other looked him up and down and said, "Thou'd ha' luked better if thoo'd had it made to fit!"

F. Austin Hyde (1957)

3
THE
WRITTEN WORD

THE BRONTËS OF HAWORTH

MORE literary pilgrimages are still made to Haworth than to all the other show places in the county together. To the average reader, the Brontës *are* Yorkshire, and Haworth Parsonage supersedes York Minster in importance. This surely is carrying hero-worship too far. More ink has probably been spilled about the three famous sisters (and their infamous brother) than about any other English author since Shakespeare, and the stream of American visitors to the shrine shows no signs of decreasing.

Gratifying as this adulation is, it is ludicrous to suggest that Haworth and the surrounding moors, any more than Coxwold, is the *essential* Yorkshire. The fact is that Yorkshire, the largest and most variegated county in England, is as different in its various Ridings as chalk and cheese. The Haworth country represents a relatively small part of the West Riding; the moors in that district have a hard and sombre cast, and the stone villages equally so. But Haworth bears no resemblance to the Yorkshire dales or the Yorkshire wolds or the verdant country of the vale of Mowbray, or the Howardian hills, or the northern moors and fells.

This does not in any way detract from the achievement of the Brontë sisters. Spending the greater part of their lives in that gloomy parsonage, looking on a dismal vista of tombstones rather than on the moors themselves, ill-treated and ill-nourished at school, handicapped by almost continual ill-health, and harassed by poverty, they yet contrived to create a romantic world of their own and to write their books under incredible difficulties.

No wonder that their weak-minded brother Branwell found the strain too great and sought solace at the Black Bull. A dyspeptic father and a housekeeper aunt who was a bit of a martinet, three literary sisters – two of whom at least had genius – and the other who was a kind of missionary – must have been difficult to live up to; and it is not surprising that he gave up the struggle. The subsequent regiment of critics – especially the women – have been a shade too severe on him.

For there is no escaping the fact that they were a strange household. Charlotte – the most ambitious and self-reliant – took the limelight and the lion's share of the praise, but Emily was the real genius of the family, and her solitary novel will be remembered when the rest are forgotten. For "Wuthering Heights" is *the* Yorkshire novel *par excellence*: no mock Dickensian heroics or sentimentality about this! It illumines that strange wild country like a beacon light. Character: land-scape: dialect: plot and passion – all are there, knit together in a marvellous story that has never yet been surpassed, and probably never will be. And if that were not enough to make her immortality secure, she wrote some of the most powerful poems in the English language.

Alfred J. Brown (1940)

I WORK IN THE DALES

I T has become my habit to go to Wensleydale for a week's solitary walking when a novel has reached a certain stage in my mind, and plan it out as I tramp along. For I feel that in that clear high sweet air, with the lapwings twisting and calling, and the great fells sweeping grandly around, one's thoughts are at their highest and clearest, least petty, widest ranging; on top of Stake Fell, with a strong wind blowing, I feel as if I understand my fellow-men. Accordingly, almost every corner of the valleys of Wensleydale and Swaledale is intimately interwoven, for me, with some part of one or other of my novels.

Take that beautiful quiet stretch of the Ure, so often photo-graphed, behind the grassy slope by Askrigg station, for example. I sat there the whole of one chilly spring morning, so still that the sheep cropped round me undisturbed, writing down a certain fictitious family of my invention, the Thorntons in my novel "The Spinner of the Years" – occasionally raising my eyes to draw encouragement from the charming picture of gentle stream, pines and grey stones.

It was on the steep shoulder of Wether Fell that I first perceived, after much inward wrestling, why I wanted to write the story of the Oldroyds in "Inheritance", and the view of the Ure, blue and sparkling on a sunny afternoon, from the road between Bainbridge and Worton, always reminds me of the murderers' escape in that novel, because I planned it there. The crown of the pass between Askrigg and Oxnop Gill, with its superb panorama of the sombre velvet summits of the Swaledale fells, not only solved a technical problem in the writing of "A Modern Tragedy" for me, but excited me to finish that novel and set its tone, as well.

A pouring wet descent towards Crackpot gave me the opening scene for my Roman novel, "Freedom Farewell", and that night I wrote its opening paragraphs in that fine Jacobean building, the Old Hall at Askrigg, which has since, alas, been destroyed by fire. Last spring, one wild wet morning as I climbed the swaying woods, waterfalls ahead thundering in my ears, following the Swale from Muker up to Keld, the sight of a lad on horseback splashing across the swollen stream gave me the opening incident to the new novel I am just trying to begin to write.

So I draw much more than just pleasure from the lovely serenity, the massive strength, of the Dales country; I feel for the Yorkshire Dales gratitude as well as love.

Phyllis Bentley (1939)

THOMAS ARMSTRONG
AT HOME

SINCE he began writing at the age of 35, novelist Thomas Armstrong has built up a reputation not only as a best-selling author but as the "quiet man" of the literary world. Public speaking and grand literary occasions are not

for him, though he acknowledges with a chuckle the persever-
ance of his publishers to get him to meet his readers.

"I don't like crowds," he told me. "I'm happiest in a small
gathering of friends. Besides, I feel a writer's job is to write –
not talk about his writing. I know this attitude of mine annoyed
a lot of people after the success of *The Crowthers of Bankdam*
and *King Cotton*. I began to hear they were saying I was a
snooty man – a head in the clouds type. A big head in the
clouds type," he amended with a grin.

"But I'm not like that really. I get on well with people and I
enjoy meeting them, but I also enjoy my own comforts and
my own pleasures and they happen to be here in Swaledale –
in my workhouse and in my surroundings – down by the river
or up on the moors."

In the spring and summer when the Dales are at their
loveliest, visitors often make a pilgrimage to "Lawn House"
on the off chance that they may see the author at work or
find him strolling in his fine gardens. Alas! they never do.
For Thomas Armstrong, once he has started on a book, cannot
be distracted and when visitors lean over his garden wall or
ring his doorbell he leaves them to his wife!

On the other hand he is pleased to receive the letters from
readers which come by every post, not only from all over
Britain but from the far corners of the world. "People are still
writing to me about *The Crowthers of Bankdam*," he told me,
"and some of them mention characters I have written about
but have now myself forgotten. They can't understand how a
novelist comes to forget characters that he has written so
fully about in a book. But that's how it is with me. Once a book
is finished and published I'm done with it. I never read a book
over again. I'm too busy writing another one."

"Don't imagine being a best-selling novelist makes you
vain," he warned me. "It doesn't if you live in the Dales. I once
went into Richmond to look at a fine old Jacobean window
that had been exposed during some demolition work. I was
standing in front of this window, admiring it, when a local
lorry driver came and stood by my side.

"That," I told him, "is a better piece of work than I'll ever
be able to manage with my stories and my books."

"You know, Mr. Armstrong," he answered, "you never spoke
a truer bloody word in your life."

Shirley Kaye (1964)

LEO WALMSLEY'S LOVE FOR BAYTOWN

T WO influences saved much of original Robin Hood's Bay for posterity. One was the near genius of the late Leo Walmsley, an author whose living eye for detail and whose deep feeling for the strong and stern character of the fishermen immortalised the village in literature. The other, without any doubt, is the cash resources of the incomers, often from far away, which have rescued many a crumbling old cottage and given it centuries more life.

Leo Walmsley, author of *Three Fevers*, and other autobiographical novels based on Bay, loved it mainly from afar, but with a passion that never waned. Coming to the village with his father, Ulric, an artist and photographer from Shipley in the West Riding, he grew up here among the alleys, and cliffs and scaurs, fascinated by the natural history of the area.

Leo was a wonderful character. Not only was he talented, but the most modest of men. He cared little for money, but was generous with his time and his friendship. At an age when most men have settled for a quiet life, he was writing and living in a glorious prime of golden Indian sumnmer.

I was privileged to know Leo's friendship during the last few years of his life and we corresponded regularly, mostly about t'awd spot, as he called the village. Right to the end he was a most vigorous writer and fierce battler for simplicity and honesty, the two traits he admired most.

Later [in 1963] he paid his last visit to Bay. He seemed ageless, striding about like a teenager with his hands in his grey flannel trousers. After 15 years, he was back to write his impressions of the village past and present for the *Yorkshire Post*. He loved every minute of those precious few days. His small shock-headed figure moved round the cottages, delightedly greeting old friends.

He told me in wonderment: "I experienced, there, something I have never felt before; a strange happiness, as I walked along the beach alone in the sun, and bathed at Mill Beck."

It was a benison, for in the following spring he was seriously ill. He was not able to introduce Stephanie, his wife, or Selina their daughter, to his beloved Bay in primrose time, though they came later and loved the place as dearly as he would have wished.

I think what Leo felt was a regeneration of his love for the village – a reawakening that many people who like books, the country, the calmer, less hurried way of life, as well as having an awe of the immense natural forces of the sea and the elements, can find there for themselves.

Barrie Farnill (1973)

4
HILLS AND DALES

A SPIRIT BROODS

THE moors of Haworth and Stanbury came within my range, yet these are grim moors – moors that have moods and can be harsh and depressing. But they can be stimulating, too, and at their worst, on days that are heavy with cloud and mist, or that threaten storm, there is a fierce fascination in them that quickens my pulse. A spirit broods over them: the spirit that fired the imagination of the Brontë sisters and gave birth to those strange characters that dominate their books; the spirit that flames in Grimshaw, the Haworth parson, imparting to his speech a heat that warmed the hearts of his parishioners even when it took the form of stern rebuke. I loved these moors, and the moor's well-known school-master, and the quaint characters who were his neighbours. I loved to drop down to Wycoller, and to listen to the stories and legends the old folk told of moorland happenings; and I loved to visit the spots the three sisters had loved, and to think of Emily preferring those bleak wastes to the joys of heaven!

But more remote places beckoned me. It is not very far to Grassington and to Malham; to Ingleborough and the mountainous regions beyond. There were half-day excursions at that time, and I counted the money well spent that opened up these more distant delights. And when I got there it was to discover that there was a "beyond" – a *terra incognita* that could be glimpsed from the Delectable Mountain I had reached, and that might be explored one day. It was something to live for! Something to look forward to in the dull days of winter. Bit by bit the unknown became familiar; the closed book opened – the glorious country watered by the infant Wharfe – Wensleydale, Teesdale and the gentler Nidderdale. "No foot of land do I possess" in any one of them, but they are all mine – and they may be yours.

William Riley (1946)

EXPLORING THE
FORBIDDEN DALE

T O the connoisseur of England the Yorkshire Dales call up nostalgic memories of rolling pastures, of grazing sheep patterned like snowdrops on an emerald hillside, of abbeys pointing their austere ruins Heavenwards, of busy market towns, macadamised motorways and neon-lighted road houses.

But three miles north of Todmorden, ringed in a cup of the Yorkshire Pennines which buttresses it from the county boundary, lies Noah Dale, the forgotten valley, deserted since steam power drove its sturdy hill farmers and handloom weavers to seek sustenance and lose their independence in the power mills by the scummed canals and lowland railways.

From Blackshaw Head, along a neglected moorland road, wet and offensive with clinging yellow mud, its middle eroded a yard below its former surface by the trickling water, the cart wheels, and the packhorse hooves of a bygone age, we meandered upward between blackened, broken walls. Soon the last habitation had been passed and the final evidences of man's modern struggle with the sour earth, a rattling corrugated sheet, a swaying loop of rusty barbed wire, had been left behind.

The wind sighed and brought a drizzle of warning. Hastily we donned our shoes and stockings, but the demons of Black Hameldon were not to be robbed of their sport. As we threw away our unfinished sandwiches and sped by the side of the stream, the gloom deepened, the thunder trumpeted and a bitter rain lashed us on our way. Through bog and swamp we squelched, oblivious of footwear and trouser bottoms, till, at last, the stream brought us, weary and sodden, below the tree line and to signs of the conquest of man. We stumbled on past ruined water mills and weed choked dams to the outskirts of Hebden Bridge.

The wind ceased. The rain, with a last flicker of contempt, soared above us to loop and return to its Pennine master.

Dripping and mud soaked, we limped into the town centre where the sun shone on the dry pavement. As we sat on the wall by the picture house waiting for a bus, an Ancient approached and, pointing to my son, asked me contentiously, "Hast thou hed no more sense than to tak' a lad of 'is age up Noah Dale to sit an' stare at Hameldon?"

"T'weather forecast said it were bahn to be a fine day," I bridled at his censure.

He frowned, glanced round anxiously to see that he was not overheard, waved his stick in the direction from which we had come and whispered in a spine-chilling croak, "Up theer lad, is t' roof of England wi' burial circles of Ancient Britons 't lived thahsands o' years sin'. Bones there are up theer, an' skeletons, an' spirits 'at walked long afore Saint Paulinus set 'is stall up at York. There's things 'appen up Noah Dale an' on Black Hameldon, queer things, 'at nawther thee nor these fancy weather forecasters 'll ivver be able to mak' head nor tail of. Thee tak' my tip, lad. Tak' t' child on a rocket to t' mooin if tha's a mind. But tha's been warned. Don't thee tak' 'im up theer ageean to sit an' stare at Hameldon."

Harry East (1963)

FAVOURITE YORKSHIRE HILLS

(Winning entries in a *Dalesman* competition)

KISDON

THERE are pansies on Kisdon, yellow and purple, fluttering a welcome as we breast the final slope. The stony pathway from Keld, leading upwards over its diminutive bridge, which spans a purling beck, has lost itself among lichen-covered birches and sturdy sycamores.

Kisdon is a friendly hill. A cuckoo calls from the scrubland around the old Hewker Lead Mines on its lower slopes – to be answered by the bubbling call of a curlew rising up from the peaty bents on Kisdon's flattened summit. The bird passes overhead, its long bill questingly pointed towards the bulk of Great Shunner etched against the south-western sky.

Away towards the north, the white walls of *Tan Hill Inn* gleam a greeting – a lonely sentinel against the wild hills of Stainmore. Opposite, the great gash of Swinnergill discharges its cascading waters into the Swale, to join the swirling rush of Kisdon Force way below.

The pathway leads downwards to the junction of the Pennine Way, and we view the sweep of the alpine-like valley formed by the northern slopes of Kisdon and the fretted crags of Ivelet Side beyond the Swale.

Around Kisdon's feet are cradled its nurslings – Muker, Thwaite and Keld – the inhabitants of which have known days of shine and shadow in their long story, like the protecting hill above them.

W.M. Newbold

ROSEBERRY TOPPING

ROSEBERRY Topping overlooks the hamlet of Newton-under-Roseberry. The Topping, highest of the Cleveland Hills, brings back many memories of my youth. As a child, it was the treat of the year to be taken to Great Ayton on a Sunday School outing. Dear old Roseberry Topping was our mecca.

We ran up and down the well-worn paths and on reaching the topmost pinnacle surveyed beautiful countryside all around. We looked down upon Airyholme Farm where, when we had clambered down the "topping", we were to have a lovely tea.

Roseberry Topping is not quite a mountain, as part of the "topping" has crumbled away under the pressure of many feet. Yet Roseberry is timeless. Many more wayfarers and explorers will ascend this highest point of the Cleveland Hills, their eyes resting upon the monument erected to a great explorer and native of Yorkshire, Captain Cook, before their gaze is held by the beauty of rolling countryside.

When travelling home from the South, Roseberry Topping is a welcome landmark. Seeing it I know I am truly a Yorkshire-woman and that "home" is among the Cleveland Hills.

E. Earle

WINDER

MY favourite hill in Yorkshire is Winder, one of the rounded hills in the Howgill Fells. Two years ago my husband and I spent a fortnight in Sedbergh. We could see Winder from a bedroom window of the guest house. We decided that on the first promising day we would climb it. We had to wait over a week. A day dawned sunny, but Winder had a misty cap. Would it clear? We decided to take the risk. We climbed slowly, for it was very steep and a chattering stream cheered us on. We stopped frequently to admire the view and in no time at all Sedbergh was below and we were looking across those two lovely dales – Garsdale and Dentdale.

It was a day when sunshine and shadow chased each other over the hills and fields. We plodded on and before long we topped the rise. In another 200 yards we were on the summit. Spread out before us was the Lake District, and we were able to recognise several mountains.

A shower of rain made up hurry downwards. It had been a winderful day, but the greatest satisfaction was that I, 60-years-old and grandmother of five, had made the walk with comparative ease.

M. Barraclough
(1972)

ENCHANTED GROUND

THE road we take is the white ribbon which climbs, like a ladder set against a roof, up and over the high slopes of a side valley. The beck which flows in its bottom is Cowside Beck. If you continue on this track, you will enjoy a steep climb and some unforgettable views over Littondale – that shy valley of the hanging woods and the brown river.

But if you want a rarer experience leave the road and follow the beck into the winding and rapidly-closing ravine. It is a deep cleft (the road upon its brow follows the 1,300 foot contour) and it will be rough going. You will be fording the water before long, wading its swift leaping shallows or springing across from stone to stone. It is not a progress for the asthmatic or arthritic. But provided you can be just a little nimble on occasion and can get over a dry-stone wall without bringing it down or leaving high priorities of your attire behind, nothing need deter you from the traverse of Cowside.

Here is enchanted ground. There are tree-encircled pools of a perfect beauty which words could only dull. There are waterfalls on exquisite settings and one which has a strange pagan loveliness that is hardly of earth at all. You must mount the steep hillside to discover its magic and it is like an approach to some haunted solitude where the old gods dwell. And then you will see a silver stream, descending a stairway of miniature terraces, in which each step is a perfect rock pool margined by tiny ferns and flowers, whose starry circlets are mirrored in the clear water. The spirit of the place is very near. You could almost believe that those drops upon the rocks, those bent grasses, mark the path of the naiads who fled as you came, clumsy-footed, up the hill.

Nearing the head of the valley its slopes become gentler and presently the fast-running stream broadens over the shallows of a wide basin amid the hills. The stones of the beck are peach-coloured here. They seem to give their damask colour to the tinkling water.

It is a quiet place. There is no human habitation in sight in all that empty landscape. Old walls follow their strange serpentine paths to far skylines. A hawk hangs motionless high overhead – then sweeps away like a blown leaf to quarter a distant hill. The silence is vibrant with the pulse of the small hidden life of the rocks and the grasses. The note of a cowbell far away, or the rattle of stones as cattle come down to drink, are notes which fall resonantly into the well of that deep peace.

Victor Allen (1951)

ON A NORTHERN MOOR

It's nobbut a year sin' thoo stood amang heather.
Gazin' awhile on far glishy hills,
Harkin' to lilts o' laverock an' chatty
An' sangs of a brace o' rush-hidden rills.

Today, I am wheer we yance stood together,
Luvin' it Darlin' as thoo used to do,
An' I am thankfu' at each year this moor
Is bee-luved, when black-ling is buddin' anew.

We nane o' us ken much aboot a Hereafter,
But some o' us do hod 'at t'Lord God is king,
'At moors, like them 'at we shared on this Earth,
Somehow, Hereafter, we surely shall find.

glishy – weathered by rain and sun.   *Dorothy Una Ratcliffe (1965)*
chatty – wheatear.
black ling – *Calluna vulgaris.*
hod – hold.

5
TOWN
AND VILLAGE

SHAPING OUT IN KEIGHLEY

K EIGHLEY is traditionally cantankerous, suspicious of change, and resisted every 19th century measure designed to ease its rawer edges. An impoverished, working-class community, too rapidly growing at the call of local cotton and worsted industries, greeted any controversy with a spontaneous disruption into lawlessness and disorder, and was by turns anti-Poor Law Amendment Act, anti-Baths and Wash-houses, anti-School Board, anti-Compulsory Vaccination...

The future poses a massive question-mark: can Keighley, by a proliferation of varied specialised industries, survive the decline of its staple textiles and engineering?

Not that there is any point in sentimentalising the past. Much of the town's demolition during the last four decades has been wholly admirable, being of the meanest slums; but sadly, too many good things have disappeared also in a general exuberance of bulldozing – our pleasant little original Mechanics' Institute, our *Queen's Theatre*, our 18th century *Fleece Inn*, the Stockbridge toll-house, even a scatter of iron Victorian urinals.

We boast, now, a fine new pedestrian precinct, highly convenient, whither, we are told, people come even from Lancashire on Saturdays to do their shopping; but somehow it all looks rather like everybody else's new precinct.

It's the same with the townsfolk. Keighley used to be famous for its characters, rejoicing in soubriquets like Old Three-Laps, Dicky Two-Pails, Emily Matchbox, Johnny Touchwood, the Whistling Dummy. Of course, only the passage of time lends them quaintness – their oral mythology, rough yet not unkind, has much to do with former deprivations, poverty, ignorance and mental deficiency.

And yet, without them, and without a battery of less flamboyant but nonetheless blunt, individualistic, energetic, didn't-care-if-they-put-their-foot-in-it citizens whom history too often forgets, aren't we perhaps, in some way, a diminished race?

Fundamentally, I don't think so. If you look closely at Keighley folk (and you may have to look hard), you'll find, underneath a vacant veneer of pubs, bingo and betting-shops, the warm comradeliness of grey close-knit streets and neighbourly backyards, together with a homely resilience.

"What are you doing?" a man was asked, in an old Keighley joke. He was down on his hands and knees in the crowd at Bingley Fair.

"Oh," he replied, scrutinising legs, "I'm just looking for a Keighley chap!"

Naturally, the off-comed-un needs to be told that's a joke about unfunny rickets and the pitiful crooked legs so long a common Keighley feature; and beyond the rickets stretch vistas of traditional malnutrition and children working in the mills while very young.

We can laugh at nearly anything at Keighley, though not always spontaneously. Whatever happens, you have a fair chance of shaping out, in Keighley.

Ian Dewhirst (1970)

WATER SPORTS AT RICHMOND

A DAM provided a wonderful open-air swimming pool which varied in depth from two to twelve feet as one moved up the river valley from Richmond. It was flanked on one side by the lip of the dam, and beyond by its gently sloping stonework buttress which took the overflow from the pool, at times sparse, at others a scintillating cascade. The other bank was a green sward.

In the upper reaches it was bordered by the delightful wood, still to be seen, the reflection of which enhanced the beauty of the whole environment. Below the dam were two small

A Dales Winter   *Terry Logan*

Great Yorkshire Show   *Terry Logan*

Mill Bridge, Skipton   *A. Firth*

Reeth, Swaledale, from Fremington Edge   Christine Whitehead

Hutton-le-Hole

Frank & Molly Partington

Staithes Bonnet (Ann Lawson)   *John Edenbrow*

Masham Sheep Fair   *Deryck Hallam*

Lastingham, North York Moors   *Deryck Hallam*

pools, perfect for paddling, and so the facilities met all needs from those of toddlers to those of competent swimmers.

Summertime meant days and nights spent in or near the pool. Perhaps because there was less urgency in our lives then than now, sunny days seemed more frequent. We did not require our imaginations to be stimulated by the underwater adventures of television since we experienced for ourselves the delights of the underwater world. We could swim underwater as ably as on the surface and I still remember the silence, the green-yellow colouring and the reflected sunlight transmitting the surface ripples as shimmering golden lines which constantly moved over the stones and pebbles of the river bed.

The water was so clear that we could throw in a sixpence and find it without difficulty even in deep water. We swam in all circumstances: in sunshine, in rainstorms of varying intensity, sometimes so heavy that the raindrops struck the water with an explosive hiss; in periods following storms when the fresh, colder water from the catchment areas of the dale used to arrive, sometimes imperceptibly, sometimes as a surge of new water moving as a small wave over the normal surface; in rich golden brown flood water of which I've often been reminded by the peaty streams in the Scottish highlands; in the evening when the moon's reflection was softened by the water smoke which followed the heat of the day; in the blue autumnal mist of morning and night.

And the inevitable wood fire; there was always a plentiful supply of dry driftwood and dead twigs in the underwood to feed the fires. Even today the aroma of wood smoke takes me back in time to the pool. We spent weeks of days and nights camping at the pool despite the proximity of our homes. The meals, always tinned beans, were cooked and served in quite unhygienic conditions but were eaten with a satisfaction not surpassed, in my opinion, by meals since enjoyed in the finest restaurants of Soho.

None of us owned a watch. Many times we were surprised to learn after hours of swimming and other activity that it was still early morning. Raft making was simple: a few planks, or logs gathered from the woods, mounted on several five-gallon drums and tied together with rope furnished weeks of fun.

The mill race we used for our own version of the Oxford

versus Cambridge boat race. Our "boats" were wooden planks roughly shaped to a point at on end. Paddles were made from a brush handle and two roughly fashioned blades, one at each end. One boy only sat astride each plank, legs dangling in the water. The real fun of these races came from the almost impossible task of retaining one's balance.

Arthur Dawson (1967)

GRASSINGTON REVISITED

S OME forty years ago when I paid my first visit to Grassington, the motor-car was still something of a novelty in the dale, and the business people of Bradford had not yet discovered the place. The horse was still master of the dusty road and the cobbled square was seldom without its waiting gigs and traps; the "Grassington Theatre" – a barn in which the great Edmund Keane and his players had once acted – was still standing.

The highlight of the summer months was the playing of the Town Band in the Square once a week, whilst the Saturday night dance at the Mechanics' Institute always drew a packed house. In those days, dancing was tackled with rare gusto and plenty of fun – and dust.

That is a long time ago, and, in the meantime, a full and active life has made names and figures somewhat blurred, but incidents still remain crystal-clear in memory.

The comparative isolation of the dale in those days produced some rare old "characters", but their picturesque individualism has been replaced by a more average stock type. I remember having my hair cut, seated in a chair in the open outside his shop, by the village cobbler. But he was much more than that. Above his window of brass-nailed clogs, a boldly-lettered board informed the world that he was a –

Clogger, Tonsorial Artist, Antiquarian, Poet,
Chiropodist, Phrenologist, Botanist –

and other vocations I have now forgotten. I can see him now; a heavy man with a cavalry moustache; never too busy for a chat or even a serious conversation.

In early 1919 I was a civilian again. I felt I must have a quiet holiday to get my bearings again, and instinctively my thoughts turned to Grassington. I went there – alone. The loveliness of Wharfedale in that perfect June, after the filth and mud of Flanders, is something I shall remember all my life. The peace and serenity of it all, the hedges pink with wild rose, and the noisy jackdaws building in the rugged limestone cliffs, the liquid gurgle of the river through fields yellow with butter-cups, the cloud shadows chasing across the fellside, and the mournful cry of the curlew – Wharfedale was never so enchanting I thought.

Grassington had changed, or perhaps I had. Many old faces had gone – some never to return. The motor-car had arrived and there was talk of a bus service up the dale; nearly every house had electric light and – it was all different somehow. The old sleepy Grassington had gone – for good. But the genuine Yorkshire welcome was there, so they overlooked the fact that I was a Lancashire man and included me in the invitation to all the boys back from the war to that memorable gathering held in the grounds of Netherfield Hall. "It were a reet do" – and that is all that needs to be said about that meeting of the dalefolk, their sons and daughters.

Since then my wanderings have led me to many other parts of Yorkshire, but not until last summer did I renew acquaint-ance with that still-cobbled Square with its old iron pump. I found a few modern fronts to old shops, a telephone exchange and an eruption of newish red-roofed villas – a red roof in a grey stone Yorkshire village should be a penal offence – but substantially the outward appearance was that of the old Grassington. I shall *have* to return sometime. The Grass Woods are still there; the moors still echo the peremptory *go-bak* of the grouse; the lively Wharfe still slithers and fumes over the water-worn rocks of the Ghaistrills; and the round cheerful face of "Fresh-air" Stubbs will still be there to welcome me to his hostelry whenever I cross his threshold again.

Norman Ellison ("Nomad" of the BBC) (1949)

EASTERTIME
AT BOROUGHBRIDGE

A S Eastertime approached, the village of Borough-
bridge stirred itself into a hive of bustling activity.
Each Thursday, a wagonette drawn by two horses
made the journey to Ripon market. Our family usually helped
to fill it for last minute shopping on Maundy Thursday.

On Good Friday morning, the baker's boy, who made his
round between seven and eight, was hailed with delight. The
hot-cross buns were warm from the oven. We ate them for
breakfast, piled high with fresh farm butter. Fish was for
lunch, of course. It was prepared before we set out along the
little old lane for church.

There was no fair for us on Easter Saturday. The only time
we went to one was Barnaby in June. Occasionally, on the
evening of Easter Saturday, we would enjoy a magic lantern
show in the village hall.

On Easter Sunday morning, we youngsters dashed to the
hen huts and gathered baskets full of eggs. They were taken
warm from the nests. I always felt that the hens, and the
strutting cockerel knew that this was a very special day. They
kicked up the dust, and crowed and clucked, seemingly in
springtime praise.

After breakfast was cleared, we donned our "Sunday best"
and went to church again. The small greystone building looked
beautiful at any time of the year, but I thought it especially
enchanting at Christmas and Easter. Daffodils proudly arrayed
on the window ledges enlivened the gloomy interior.

When I was seven years old, in 1908, mother looked buxomly
bonny in ankle length black and white silk dress. A huge
flower-decked straw hat was set firmly upon her greying hair.

Spring sunshine streamed through half-opened church
windows, and our family sat sedately in its usual pew. The
"toffs" up at the front of the church included Lady Lawson
Tancred and Doctor Dagett. Father's voice was gruff with
emotion as, straight as a ram-rod, he swelled the jubilant
chorus of 'Jesus Christ is Risen Today' – and mixed his
Alleluja's up hopelessly!   *Hilda M. Haigh (1980)*

LIFE IN THE VILLAGE O' QUEER FOAK

I WAS not aware that I had taken up residence in the Village o' Queer Foak until some six months after I had settled in. Then one morning during a stroll in the upper reaches of the Dale, I engaged in conversation with a brown-faced man who was busy gap-walling. "Wheer didta say tha'rt livin'?" he asked.

I told him and he grinned. "Oh ah! That's a reet place that is. We ca' it the village o' Queer Foak – they're reet queer, yon lot."

Lots of queer things happened, or rather did not happen. One of these was the annual parish meeting. I had tried for several years to find out when and where it was held. After some enquiry, I found out who was the chairman and when I asked him about the meeting, he was evasive. "You'll see th' notice up like anyone else," he said.

"But where do you put it up?"

"Ha! That's summat else you'll ha' t' find out."

Eventually I did find out. He used to pin up the notice inside his barn door, and kept the door shut. I also found out that if I could get six people on the electoral roll we could demand a meeting. Again I approached the chairman, and told him if nothing was forthcoming, we would lay it before the R.D.C. That shook him. He gave us the date and place of the next meeting. We told him we were going to propose a new chairman and also new trustees of the village charities.

The village began to boil. We were not very popular. Dark and dirty were the looks, but we went ahead. The meeting was held in the chairman's house, illegal according to the by-laws, but we let that pass. Fifteen of us squashed into a small room, and the chairman rose to open the meeting. No minutes were read, for the simple reason that there had been no parish meeting for many years.

"T' first thing," said the chairman, "is about this brass in t' charities. What are we t' do about that?"

"How much is there in it?" someone asked. The treasurer stood up, "Sixty-odd quid, and I'm resigning the job."

"Any suggestions?" asked the chairman.

"I propose we split it among the old age pensioners," said one of the village elders. The chairman and treasurer were also pensioners. The vote was unanimous.

"Now that's settled," said the chairman. "I'm resigning too." He sat down only to rise again quickly. "I nominate my son to be chairman." We immediately nominated one of our own party. Both were seconded.

"Awreet, hands up all those i' favour of my lad." We protested against a show of hands. Illegal, we argued. There must be a secret ballot for chairman. After some bickering, we won our point. The ballot showed seven for our nominee and the same for his son. The chairman hadn't voted. The old man didn't know he had the casting vote. "Now what're we bown t' do?" he asked.

"Toss up for it," I suggested. They refused. At length it was agreed that his son should be chairman for six months and our nominee for the six months after. His son took over the minute book and said: "The meeting's closed. There's no other business."

I don't know if they still hold Parish meetings in our village. I have never enquired. Sometimes when I'm in the local having a pint and someone mentions democracy, I wonder if I should invite them to attend. I have lived here twenty years now and it's still the Village of Queer Foak. Should any Dales visitor park his car on the verge to admire the view, he is liable to be ordered to go on his way by one of our Queer Foak. They say i' Lancashire – "All the world is queer but me and thee, and sometimes I think tha's a bit queer."

"Off-Cummed-Un" (1969)

6
COTTAGE WAYS

LIVING UNDER THATCH

I N Old Malton there are houses with roofs of red pantiles, slates and even corrugated iron, but three cottages always invite special attention, for their roofs are made of wheat straw. The straw is not new and yellow, but old, ragged, tired-looking. Sparrows chirp excitedly around it, for the edges hold out great possibilities at nesting time, and where a stray seed, carried by the wind, has lodged among the brittle stems you can see a shaft of fresh green in Spring.

The folk of Old Malton favoured thatched roofs long after other villages had a canopy of red tiles. I like the tiles, and there is no finer sight in the North Riding than a fine sweep of green and brown country, gently wooded, with islands of red

here and there which are the towns and villages. But I also like thatched cottages. There is nothing harsh about them, and in this age of concrete and tubular steel they are enchanting.

Fifty years ago there were over twenty thatched cottages in Old Malton. Today the number is three, with another only partly thatched. There were eight thatched cottages on the Malton side of the village, five in Chapel Lane, two near the school and five on the Pickering side. William Bradley and Tom Freer were thatchers here within memory.

Robert Postill lives at a thatched home which was once known as Rose Cottage but now has a number on the door. It is 89 years since his father became the tenant, and Robert was born there 74 years ago. He told me: "If thatched cottages are looked after, they'll last donkey's years. There was talk of them pulling my place down, but Government said it had to stop. This is a good cottage for such as me. It's well looked after. I whitewashes it every year, outside and in, though it's about seven years since a new thatching was put on. It was patched up about two years ago. When William Bradley was thatching, roofs lasted fifteen years. He charged 3s. a day. And, by the way, when I started work I'd £5 for t'year."

"It's all right living under thatch as long as it's kept in repair," says Mr. Postill. "Course, you gets birds' nests in thatch; they used to wire 'em so that birds couldn't nest, but I blocked the holes up with bagging. Best way to get shut o' birds is to roost 'em out on a night."

He lives by himself. In summer time the thatch is cool; in winter it keeps the house warm. "When you get in here on a frosty night and get doors shut up an' fire made up, you have to sit back, I can tell you." Once his father had the services of an uncle, and the house was re-thatched in five days and a half. "That job cost Dad 18s.," said Mr. Postill.

As I walked down the street I felt it was a pity that this pleasant North Yorkshire village is gradually losing its thatched homes. In a few years they will only be a memory. As I plodded towards the new Malton over the hill I heard the gay chirruping of sparrows busy nesting in the warm and friendly thatch of a cottage. There will be a housing shortage for sparrows when the last of these grand old buildings is demolished.

Fred Metcalfe (1953)

LOST COMFORTS

MOST old Dales' dwellings have walls that are at least two feet thick and so afford maximum insulation. The small, well-fitted windows are ideal for conserving warmth and so are the thick well-fitting doors. The greatest aid to conserving heat in the old days was the thatched roof. Tiles and slates have extremely poor insulating properties; thatch affords the maximum. When thatch went out of fashion and slates and tiles took its place a great deal of winter comfort was lost.

The ventilation of the old-time dwelling was extremely efficient. Well-fitting doors and windows guarded against draughts. The shape and size of the open hearth enabled a large volume of air to be heated, and the chimney, sloping up to a narrow outlet, gave an adeqate, but not excessive air change, with the peat and wood fuel then in use.

The ceilings of these old houses played an important part in ventilation and distribution of heat. There were no plaster ceilings in those days and warm air rising constantly from the heated living rooms kept the bedrooms beautifully warm and dry without any need for upstairs heating. The thatch above prevented this heat from leaking away too quickly.

The absurd fashion of covering the ceiling of the living rooms with a lath and plaster ceiling in imitation of town houses completely upset the balance of ventilation and the distribution of heat. It induced too much draught up the chimney and cut down the supply of heat to the bedrooms with the result that such rooms, already deprived of the protecting thatch, became cold and damp and had a temperature only a few degrees above that of the outside air. From the point of view of comfort and health it was a sheer disaster. The bedrooms of the old-time Dales' farmers were as comfortably heated as those of a modern luxury flat.

The gathering of peat and wood against the winter may have been a sore burden to the Dalesfolk and one can well understand the desire to be rid of this burden by the installation of coal-burning grates, but the heating of the dwelling suffered in consequence. Peat with its slow burning properties was the ideal fuel. The fire could be made up at night and would burn gently without attention till the morning. So, through the coldest hours the dwelling was kept warm and the inmates slept in constantly warmed bedrooms. When they got up in the morning there was no need to come down to a chilly room and kindle a fire; they came down to a warm room and just topped up the heat quickly by flinging a few pieces of wood on to the fire.

In days gone by the cosy cottage in the country was a comfortable substantial fact, and not what it is to-day – a pleasant fiction. If I could I would put the clock back, for in my opinion, coal fires, slate roofs and nice white ceilings are poor recompense for the comfort that has been lost.

H. Bryce Thompson (1947)

MIND THAT JUG!

T HERE is something symbolic about the sneck of a Dales bedroom door. It is usually of the vast and solid proportions associated with the entrance to an ancient cathedral or an Oxford college. Perhaps, after all, it has more affinity with the cathedral than the college since when one lifts the sneck it is to claim sanctuary for a brief while from the troublesome outer world, much as did the mediaeval fugitives from the law when they grasped the handle of the church door. Yet having closed the door behind you it may be that you have shut out one set of troubles only that others will soon manifest themselves.

Beds in these rooms vary from those into which you fit much as a mummy in a sarcophagus to those into which you sink, if not into the slough of despond, at least into an apparently bottomless pit like some form of feather Buttertubs, with the result that next morning you need all the arts of the speleologist in order to extricate yourself. And from the bed to the customary washstand is often but an elbow's reach. There stand, the bane of every Dales visitor's life, the large, shallow wash basin and the large and anything but shallow water-jug or ewer. Call it what you will. The richest vocabulary of abuse couldn't do justice to it. Solid though it may appear the common ewer has the fragility of a soap-bubble and on the slightest provocation proceeds to flood the room as though

Mill Gill beck in spate had come in through the window. It will probably run over at the first pouring and nothing short of seizing all the bed clothes and curtains and stripping yourself to the skin will provide sufficient material to act as floor-cloths before the overflow makes itself felt downstairs.

If the bowl doesn't overflow danger still lurks. Unless you've poured the water into the bowl with it standing on the floor, which is not easy, you'll have to lift it down from the wash-stand. An easy operation were it not that the particular form of china, or porcelain, from which these utensils are manu-factured is polished to an insane degree of smoothness by some pottery workers with a grudge against Dales ramblers. Accordingly it will slip from your fingers with the dexterity of an eel and break as easily as an egg shell.

Dressing-table drawers stick hard and strike you as being

so immovable that it is difficult to believe that they are not, like the excellent shelves of books in so many stage-sets, just painted on for effect. Just as you decide to hang everything over a chair, or if you are not fastidious, to put them, as an old Yorkshireman used to say to me, "on t' dog shelf" (floor), these drawers fly open and propel you backwards as though you'd been thrown in a bout of Cumbrian wrestling. Then, after you've assiduously read the faded sheets of "The Craven Herald", the "Darlington and Stockton Times", or the "Westmorland Gazette" which line the drawers, you can safely put your clothes away.

On the chest of drawers or dressing-table is a mirror. Handle it as you would the wash-basin and jug – as though it were quicksilver. This mirror is of the swinging variety and its worst enemy could not accuse it of not properly fulfilling its function. As to whether it swings where required is another matter.

Yet, of even the most disconcerting of Dales bedrooms may it be said "with all thy faults I love thee still." Like the Yorkshireman himself they are the better for knowing. And they have one outstanding – or upstanding – virtue. Although the ceilings of Dales bedrooms may be low, they are not as consistently depressed as those of houses farther south. The size of bruise raised on the head by precipitate contact with Dales roof beams doesn't begin to compare with those inflicted by the roofs and beams of Anne Hathaway's cottage. The somewhat protuberant bulge on Shakespeare's brow, attributed by most to his intellect, was, equally likely, one of the contusions of courtship. If you compare, after extensive travel, the different county souvenirs on your cranium, you'll find that the Dales Dent is inconsiderable when compared with the Buckinghamshire Bump, the Warwickshire Weal, the Cotswold Clout or the Worcestershire Wallop.

Frank W. Dibb (1943)

WEEKEND COTTAGE

It was a mistake to buy that little house on the Fell
As a weekend retreat,
And spend the dark months there
Mending the roof and floors, and re-pointing the stone;
Buying curtain material and pots and pans
And cleaning, cleaning, cleaning
The cobwebs and mould of the silent empty years
Until all became whole and sweet again.

It was a mistake to think we should lie in peace there
Watching the sun rise over the sleeping Dale
And hearing the cocks crowing and a distant sheepdog,
And playing at house there through the long summer
        mornings –
It was a mistake to think any house could be so perfect
And (unfortunately) such a delight to our visitors,
For the house has become
A halting place,
Snack-bar,
Semi-public convenience,
Anything but our home.

We air the bedding for people who have more time to
        retreat than we,
Order the milk, leave the key at the Pub, and rush back
        to town
Where we are expected to attend
The Rotary Club,
Visit the sick,
Give a talk on Country Life at the Ebenezer Chapel,
Or otherwise just go on
Working, working, working.

Oh, yes, it was a mistake to ever have thought of retreating
        to the Fell –
For what you never had you never miss,
Oh, well!

                                    Joan Pomfret (1969)

7
LIFE AND
TRADITION

CUCKOO CALLS
THE PEAT-CUTTERS

PEAT is the point of my story. For 76-year-old Mr. Leeming and his wife of 69 – grand dalesfolk intoning that soft burr of the Bowland country – are peat-cutters. Not in any grandiose commercial way, mark you, but according to the dwindling tradition of the prudent cottager. When the cuckoo first calls, on 26th April or thereabouts, this genial couple take wheelbarrow, spades and turfing tools four miles to a favourite turf-pit on Croasdale Fell in quest of winter fuel.

There are several kinds of turfing tool, but the one they favour resembles a spade with the centre of the blade "fretted out" and a tiny cutting edge fixed at right angles to one side. It is a sharp instrument and is used with a horizontal thrust, the little upright flange gauging the thickness of the turves, usually about an inch and a-half.

Maybe there's a knack in it. But Mr. Leeming, who began cutting peat for his father at Dale Head when he was thirteen, assured me with a chuckle that he could teach me the trade in a matter of hours.

The Leemings generally spend a month getting their peat. A fortnight's hard work would suffice, because in a normal winter when coal deliveries are regular they use peat only as a supplementary fuel, but they prefer to make a pleasure of the job. Dalespeople reckon it needs fifty cart-loads of peat to keep a cottage fire going all the year round. And I am not referring to the almost-extinct system of perpetual combustion in "bowl grates", where, as Mrs. Leeming recalls, potatoes were roasted in the ash.

These Slaidburn folk usually work peat to a depth of four or five feet after the top sod has been lifted (it is possible to go six feet and deeper); the turves are laid flat on the ground to dry and afterwards stacked in "hubs". In a good season the peat will dry in a fortnight, but there have been times when the Leemings have had to leave their peat out on the moor till the following spring.

There is good and bad peat. Properly selected and dried, however, it gives a good uniform heat, burns brightly and cleanly. I have never sat by a cosier fire than the one I saw at Dene Cottage.

The hard winter has set many Bowland people seriously to think of utilising the rich peat seams at their doors. "There are tons of peat on the fells," Mr. Leeming told me, "and since the motor-lorry has solved the old problem of transport, I don't see why peat-cutting should not be developed on a large scale."

R.R. Waterhouse (1947)

THE SEWING BEE

W ELL, now, Sarahanna Holroyd was getting married so all we girls had to help her to sew hems on her sheets and help to make pillowslips. In those days only rich folk could afford to buy sewing machines, so poorer folk helped each other with their hand sewing, especially before a lass got married.

When Sarahanna was getting married we had a "Sewing Bee" at her house to hem her sheets. Sarahanna's mother had lighted a big fire in their parlour, so there we sat and sewed, very cosy and warm.

To pass the time on, and help us to sew better, we sang all our songs, and bits out of the *Messiah*, or whispered gossip together. Sarahanna was a good teller of ghost stories, and Agnes Maude Gedge, whose father was our choir master and taught singing, sang some lovely songs like *Put My Little Shoes Away*, or *Close The Shutters, Willie's Dead*. Our favourite was a new song called *Just a Song at Twilight*. Agnes sang it beautifully and we all joined in the chorus.

When the fire had burnt low, Sarahanna's mother popped her head round the door and said: "Come on, lasses, leave your sewing for now, and have your suppers."

We all went into the big kitchen and there on the large kitchen table was set our supper. We all sat down to a plate of cold meat, eaten with slices of home made bread, and pickles of all sorts: piccalilli, red cabbage, pickled cauliflowers and little onions. Sarahanna's mother was noted for her pickles.

We finished off with apple pasty and cheese, washed down with a small glass of home brewed beer. It was very potent and was a pale golden brown, very sharp and cool.

As we left the house, Sarahanna's grandma passed round a square tin of broken pieces of treacle toffee which she'd been making over the fire all the time we'd been sewing. When it was ready she'd poured it to cool off into a well-greased flat Yorkshire pudding tin. When it was cooled she'd broken it into pieces for us to suck and eat as we went home – a sort of thank-offering for our sewing.

Mary E. Cooper (1965)

AUNT SABINA'S FUNERAL

THE thin string of mourners slowly and painfully climbed the steep hill to the church. The farm wagon which bore Aunt Sabina had been cleaned up and looked much too festive in its bright blue and orange paint. The coffin rested on Aunt's hearthrug. It was a new rug, with patches of purple and red in it. She had been keeping it these two years for a special occasion.

Now and again the humble procession paused to rest, for it was a hot day. Aunt Helen looked uncomfortable in her borrowed black which was a bit tight; Mrs. Gaybody's style was certainly not hers. We came to a standstill again under the beech tree half way up the hill.

"Summat's up," said Cousin Jim in a respectful whisper. "Bell's not tolling."

At last we arrived at the churchyard gate, village folk and stray relations joining us there. According to custom the Vicar should have met us here and, chanting, led us into church. But no parson was to be seen! What was to be done? We waited and waited, registering the proper emotion expected of us on such a solemn occasion, but not a sight of parson was there. After the family conclave carried on in anxious mutterings and low growlings the undertaker went off to seek him, and we all moved into the welcome shade of the trees.

What a "ter do" to be sure. None of us would have been in the least surprised to see Aunt Sabina, with her sharp nose and beady eyes, pop out her head and demand in that shrill voice of hers "What is he waitin' for?" She was always in a hurry. Cousin Jim, who was a timid man, plaintively squeaked that "it would 'a been a sad day for all on us if Aunt 'ad bin at wrong side o' t' coffin."

"My, this would make a stir in t' place," they said. "The worst of it is you never know wi' parsons and t' like what they're up to. Had it been anybody else in t' village you've a good idea where they'd be and what they're doing at any given time."

"Mother," I said, "I know a likely place," and glad to be released I ambled off down the steep path to the beck.

Reaching the edge of the steep bank I peered down through the trees and, sure enough there was the Rev. Mr. Ford enjoying himself immensely. Minus shoes and socks he sat there with a book and a bottle of Brussell's cooler handy. Yes, he was fishing. I watched breathlessly as he landed a beauty.

"Mr. Ford," shouts I. "It's Aunt's funeral."

"Bless my soul, so it is. I'd forgotten! Dear! dear! and your Aunt always so impatient. What a pity! what a pity! – and the trout rising well this afternoon. Tell them I'm coming, and toll the bell."

I tolled the bell, though mother said it was more like a wedding than a funeral.

"Ashes to ashes and dust to dust," chanted the parson, scattering the good soil on Aunt Sabina's coffin. He was scarcely through when Uncle Ben uplifts his voice and shouts to all and sundry – "There's a grand tea waiting at 'White Hoss'. Ivverybody's welcome!"

Margaret Winter (1951)

HAVE YOU SEEN
A "HOOKY" RUG?

HOOKY rugs demand a setting – a high, narrow mantel-shelf, flanked at each end by heavy brass candlesticks, then, moving in a place, a pair of black and white, or gold and white, china dogs, then moving in again, doll-sized furnishings in brass or copper – a fender, a chair, a kettle.

The fireplace itself must be a shining blackleaded range, its oven embellished with gleaming steel, a side boiler balancing it, and the high, barred grate between. Immediately in front of the hooky rug comes a formidable array of fire irons in polished brass or steel, resting on a heavyweight fender in the same metal, all on a spotless, whitewashed hearth, with a high, black, brass-topped tidy Betty to keep in falling cinders.

Then the hooky rug looks right, its thickness excluding draughts that might sneak over the flags or shining lino of the floor, its four-inch black border setting off the medley of colours within.

Thirty years ago, as soon as the nights drew in, my mother began her yearly winter's task of rugmaking. All through the year old clothes had been carefully saved or begged, preserved from the moths in camphor balls. Black was particularly sought after, for the regulation border.

At one time, when everyone's best was "a good black", this was probably easily come by. But as this fashion declined it became increasingly difficult to find enough material to cut into the long, inch wide strips that were again clipped into four-inch lengths with cross corners to prevent fraying.

I was allowed to do this second cutting, and the "clips" were stored in a clean sack. The new rug went down after spring cleaning and lasted till the following spring, when it was relegated to the back kitchen.

Inside the black border, artistic taste was allowed to run riot. I remember a red ring in the centre with red rays marching out in every direction, and a red quarter circle in each corner – the result of an old red dressing-gown. Many was the game of "taws" we played on that rug the next winter, using the red ring in the centre as the hole, when the originally upright "clips" has been long since flattened with constant treading. But the *pièce de résistance* was the rug with the bunch of deep pink roses in one corner. Originally they were a flannel khaki army shirt, dyed pink and transformed into a warm winter frock for me, and lastly and most gorgeously the bunch of pink roses in the new hooky rug. The dark green leaves were identifiable as an old winter coat. To sit and look at a hooky rug could invoke as reminiscent a mood as a patchwork quilt.

M.A. McManners (1961)

SALE FEVER

*Now Spring is here and daffies nod
And furtive weeds peep from the sod
Now April sun blinks through the rain
'Tis time to go to sales again.*

*No, not to join the city queues
For shirts reduced and half-price shoes,
But with your friends to see them selling
The contents of some rural dwelling:*

*The chairs and tables, mirrors, clocks,
And odds and ends in cupboard box,
The paintings – people never cease
To hope will be some masterpiece.*

*There folks drop in to search for treasure,
The keener ones with book and measure,
Their kids let loose to run and rummage
Or on the carpets have a scrummage.*

*Upon a table 'waiting bids
Lie pans and teapots with no lids,
Saucers many, cups too few,
But if you're lucky something new.*

The sale begins, the dealers vie
To catch the auctioneer's eye,
And woodworm in the chairs turns pale
At emigrating from the dale.

As "Antique" fever strikes the throng
The prices leap, the bidding's long,
And things that Gran used every day
Are destined for the U.S.A.

The gavel strikes its final blow,
The audience begins to go
Back home, the prices reached to tell,
And attics search for goods to sell.

Helen Pierson (1977)

8
THE NATURAL
WORLD

GEESE OVER HUMBER

IT was low tide on the Humber estuary that first Sunday afternoon in October. Faxfleet was bathed in warm autumn sunshine and downstream the huge expanse of Whitton Sands lay bare. All was peace and quiet on this mile and a quarter wide refuge for wildfowl.

Small parties of ducks were taking off at short intervals, disappearing inland into the night. A rhythmical swooshing from behind filled the air as six swans flew out over the remaining floating birds. Finding no resting ground they continued round in a circle to retreat back up the canal.

A warm pink glow filled the eastern sky as the full moon rose on the estuary, shimmering its golden light across the waters and growing brighter each minute. Way out over the Lincolnshire hills came an unmistakable honking of flying geese. Louder and louder it sounded, filling the moonlit night with the wildest of all wild music until the whole sky vibrated.

Now they were just visible in the glasses – long dark lines of pink-feet, rising and falling, altering shape continuously and gradually increasing in size. The leading birds could easily be distinguished. This must be the same party returning I thought, as I estimated around 500 birds in two separate flocks.

The geese were a good half a mile away and the last glow of sunset gone. I could just make them out through the night glasses, all closely packed together, paddling hard to keep position in the strong tide. A red navigation light on the opposite bank served as a marker, and it was obvious that the geese were not having it easy.

They were gradually losing position, drifting upstream

with the tide. In ten minutes they had lost a good hundred yards, with an hour to go before high water.

The tide was beginning to slacken, and soon they would be able to relax and take it easier, to drift back downstream and wait for the roost to re-appear above the waves. Then once more the geese could stand on terra firma, tuck their heads under a wing, take a well earned rest and sleep in the moonlight through the rest of the night, safe and sound on their island refuge.

Frank Oates (1967)

BEES TO THE HEATHER

THE early days of August see a movement of population to be counted by the million, every one of which could hum a confident "Yes" to the question – "Is your journey really necessary?" The bees are going to the moor, and among Yorkshire bee-keepers within hail of the heather there's "thrang deed".

Around Pickering, moor-time represents the chief chance of a harvest. Fruit blossom merely stimulates the hives. Clover is not so abundant as it was before the ploughing-out policy began. One man I know who often took a thousand clover sections, had not one last year. For us, all depends upon the heather.

In the old days of horse-drawn transport, moor-time meant a whole night's adventure. Now Frank motors easily up the ten miles in a few minutes. Yet these ten miles give entry to a new world – to the peaty, heathery tang of the moorland.

Dark pinewoods provide the bield from northerly winds. Grey stone walls or turf dykes shelter our immediate hive-stance, and then, stretching out for miles, the glory of the heather. The bell-heather is full out, the ling just about to break, for we like the bees to meet the flow, to know their countryside in advance. Last year when a spell of bad weather delayed the flow, hundreds of stocks were lost through lack of stores in the hives.

Ropes are slackened, the hives lifted off. "Dean't let it come doon wiv a soss! Humour it doon!" says one as the first hive is lowered.

We place them "unoddly" as one helper says, rather than in straight lines, to help the bees to locate their own hives and so prevent "drifting" – the tendency of bees to go to the end of the row when there's little difference in colour and position of hives. Entrances face to the east of south so that the early morning sun will waken the hives to life. Then we unfasten the closed porches. From some there is not a murmur. From others comes a sudden rush of angry bees and hands and ankles are viciously "tenged".

Tomorrow with the first light these countless millions, which for the past weeks have been making the lime trees hum, will come out to a new world – a world of tiny heather bells, a limitless new source of pollen and nectar. The shaking of the journey and, surely, the pure wine of the moorland air, will make them sense a new position and take new sighting flights – an amazing thing this homing power of the bees – the hive will be photographed through the myriad lenses of the workers' eyes and then in a bee-line they will be off to the heather.

F. Austin Hyde (1947)

Wagon Road Bridge, near Skipton Castle   *F. Williams*

Riders above Reeth   *S.C. Sedgwick*

Cottage at Runswick Bay   *Bernard Fearnley*

Studrigg Scar, near Austwick   D. Dakeyne

Chapel-le-Dale, near Ingleton   *D. Dakeyne*

Beamsley Beacon, from near Langbar   *Colin Raw*

Kilnsey, Upper Wharfedale   *Tom Sykes*

Home Farm at Temple Newsam, Leeds   C. Robinson

BILBERRY TIME!

SPLAT! In a moment of pure malice a wayward bird deposited a gobbet of richly purple lime straight across my new washed windscreen. My first reaction was one of furious dismay. But then I mellowed. It meant the beginning of the bilberry season.

Surely the first week of July was too early! It didn't seem long since the tiny richly pink flowers had been in full bloom. But birds have sharp eyes and keener appetites for the luscious bilberry. It would soon be time to start a-picking.

As you will gather by this time, bilberries are one of my favourite fruits, and all the better (I am a Yorkshireman after all) for being free. They do, however, exert a price, in the form of aching muscles and the danger of a slipped disc. Bilberry-picker's back, I suppose the medicos call it.

Sometimes you will see a group of people, etched out on the skyline, whirling their arms like windmill sails. They are bilberry-pickers who are trying to rid themselves of the flies. Where there are bilberry plants there are flies. But flies which live frustrated lives. There they are, ensconced among peat and green leaves with only beetles for company when all they really yearn to do is feast on human flesh. Bilberry season must spell the red-letter days of their little lives. Their favourite food not only comes to them, it conveniently leans down to be fed upon. But where is adventure without challenge!

The bilberry plant itself is intent on making things difficult. Bilberries on the sunlit uplands can be found in great numbers, but they are small pathetic fruit. You have to poke and pry, lifting the leaves and seeking out the slightly shady places where the giants among the community suck up the moisture and grow fat and succulent.

Sadly the bilberry emerges into the world at the same time as strawberries, raspberries and just about every other soft fruit you care to mention. Your hands are scratched and your back aches and you feel you never want to see another soft fruit as long as you live.

But these wild berries are tantalising. Their season is far longer than our short-lived garden fruit. Venture further up the moorland slopes and you will find new generations of bilberries springing up six weeks or more after the first ones have appeared. If the year is favourable some of the plants manage to produce a second crop as late as the beginning of September, but these tend to be rather too small for the bilberry enthusiast.

I wish you well with your picking ... but mind your back.

John Hewitt (1988)

A DOCTOR IN EVERY HEDGE

YORKSHIRE folk have always been noted for their faith in herbs. Many of our present-day remedies originated in the isolated farmhouses and cottages in the Dales. Even today it is chiefly in these rural homesteads that the herbal flag is being kept flying, the lady of the household being family doctor in times of sickness. In days when transport and communication were not as highly organised as today she was often country physician in the absence of professional attention. Beneath huge bunches of basil, sage and thyme, which hung from the rafters, she worked with pestle and mortar busily compounding some herbal medicament for a time of need, just as she daily put those same herbs to culinary use.

At certain times of the year folk could be seen combing the fields and hedgerows in search of herbs which they took home, dried and made into salves, oils, decoctions and infusions. Angelica for colds and coughs, balm for nervous headache; broom for kidney complaints; hops for nervous disorders. Pillows were stuffed with this herb and used to promote sleep when all other means failed (those who suffer from insomnia take note!).

At midsummer the stinging nettle came into its own, the village lads and lasses being employed in "plucking" the tops and extracting the juice to be used whenever the thirst required quenching. For the male members of the family who had insatiable thirsts nettle beer was brewed.

The work of the village herb seller was not confined to making up simple infusions, salves and oils. Numerous secret recipes were handed down. According to Gerard, writing in the 16th century, yarrow was given "to prevent blotches", while rosemary was regarded as being specific "as an amorous medicine to make one in love"! Bryony was used "to take away the colour of a black eye". Mistletoe was said to be good "for those that hath no delight"!

Beer being more potent than it is today, wood betony was given "to keepe a man from being drunke"! An infusion of gentian was used as an outward application "to cure copper faces"! Elder was advocated "for such as are too fat and would faine be leaner"; pennyroyal "to provide greate force against the swimming head", and vervain "for mad and furious men"!

At Christmas mistletoe was given "to make thy heart merry". Those of a sensitive nature were told to drink marigold wine "for thy wounded heart". Those who had weak muscles were given peione "to strengthen the sinews". Red sage was recommended "to fasteneth the teeth" and the great water dock "to make younge wenches look faire and cherry-like"!

In the treatment of animal complaints the "wise woman" really came into her own. Balm was advocated as an outward application for sore paws in dogs and lungwort was given for distemper. Cats when sick were given nettle juice. Dandelion was regarded as being most efficacious when given to goats "in order to improve the quantity and quality of the milk", while ground ivy was renowned for its efficacy in "keeping little dogs from growing greate"!

Kenneth Rawnsley (1955)

THE FATE OF A WOOD

ARLY on Monday morning, men and lads on cycles arrive in twos and threes. Standing round the foreman they view the scene of operations with disfavour, for it is part of the woodman's ritual never to approve of a new undertaking. The little ceremony ends with a "well lads" from the foreman whereupon the group springs into an animation which belies all recent forebodings.

Unearthing his hidden axe, each wood-faller rubs the moisture from the shaft and runs his thumb along the keen edge of the blade which, for efficiency, must be constantly ground to razor-like sharpness.

Soon axes are swinging and the wood resounds to the "chock" of the axe-mens' blows. Clean white chips fly everywhere as stark collars appear round the bases of the trees. The nature-lover stands by, fascinated in spite of himself, for he knows that the "hewing of wood" is one of the oldest crafts in the world, and one that will remain to out-live all others.

The first tree is now "spurned-up" with a deep facing on the side in which it is intended to fall. Fixing handles to the long slender blade of the saw, the woodmen kneel on the ground and commence to cut with a rhythmical grace which comes only with years of experience.

No French aristocrat faced the guillotine with haughtier calm than does a tree on its day of execution. Not until the final moment, when the woodmen call "timber" to warn those in the vicinity of the impending "drop", does the tree succumb to the death-rattle shudder which comes just before its fall – a hissing plunge, a sickening crash and then – silence.

Whilst the wood-fallers "get their wind" by an examination of the butt to see "how she's felled", the lads, with no hint of pity for the prostrate tree, commence the amputations; dexterously chopping away the branches – "dressing out" it is termed – until only the bole remains. The tree has now become an article of commerce, and as such, assumes quality and form which can appeal to the nature-lover no less than the business-minded merchant.

Meanwhile, unknown to all save the understanding nature-lover, there has commenced that first trickle of refugees, who, driven from their hardly-won hunting grounds, are forced to fight their way into the preserves of unfriendly neighbours. These in turn, as the felling advances, must join the ever-swelling stream until, after we know not what savage biological wars, they are able to settle in new and as yet unthreatened quarters.

George Jackson (1946)

9
MOVING ALONG

PACK-HORSE WAYS

EVERY Dalesman, worthy of the name, must, at some time have walked with joy and gratitude along one or other of the green roads over the fells, and in his heart poured blessings on the unknown makers of such a lovable track. The way over Horsehead into Littondale; parts of the road from Settle to Malham and forward to Kilnsey; tracks from Arkengarthdale to Bowes, and similar ways between every dale and its neighbours, are known to all who frequent the fells and moors.

A winter evening spent with adequate maps will soon reveal that those many fragments of green road and bridle path can be linked up into a few continuous ways, partly incorporated in later roads; ways often crossing the whole Dales area, and traceable even further afield, suggesting that at some time in their history they have been highways of importance used by traffic to and from far places, a traffic now lost and forgotten or shifted into the valley bottoms on to new roads and railways. Pack-horse roads and bridges, drove roads, "streets" and "gates" are memorials of a time when the byways and hamlets of today had a different importance and were vital parts of the economic life of the area.

If on some fine moonlit night we could see the ghosts of these old users of the green roads passing along them once more, what a procession we should enjoy – monk and drover, collier, charcoal burner and shepherd, salter and packman from the distant fairs, would throng by with pack ponies whose panniers held a surprising range of goods: coal, charcoal, salt, wool, and hides, perhaps would be the bulkiest; cloth, grain, small domestic ware, wooden utensils and crockery, with lead, silver, and ironware, and in the packman's or "chapman's" packs, silks, ribbons, cheap jewellery, spices and comfits, and small drapery from far distant fairs.

Along the lowland and eastward tracks between the coastal markets such as Boston and Hull and York, and the monastic houses, we should watch a traffic of wines, vestments, parchments and books, for the abbeys with delicacies for the abbot's table and lodgings, returning after the carriage of wool and lead for export to France and Italy. Macadam and Stephenson and their armies have changed all that, and drawn the traffic to the valley bottoms, leaving the highways of the fells and moors for the wandering dalesman and the hiker. Let us value our heritage all the more for the busy past it has known, in contrast with its present grateful solitude.

Arthur Raistrick (1941)

THE CARRIERS OF HOLDERNESS

BETWEEN three and four o'clock in the afternoon, the procession of carriers' carts was a familiar sight on the roads leading out of the city. Each looked like a brown square hut built on top of a farm wagon and drawn by one or two lumbering horses.

I remember the dusky December afternoons when I waited with my mother on the cold quiet suburban road for the Burton Pidsea carrier to pull steadily out of the mist. The sound of the hooves and the grind of metalled wheels were heard long before we saw the glimmer of the swinging lantern.

We'd hail the carrier and he would turn to put the parcels – presents for my aunt and cousins – carefully along the load in the cart. It was like a snug store-house in there.

The big horses would stamp and their breath shine in the lamplight. Their feet looked like soft pads because of the tufts of hair around them, but they struck sparks from the frosty ground in their strain to move away.

Sometimes in the later summer a letter would arrive from my uncle and we'd go into the town to meet another carrier whose route did not pass our lane end. We collected a box of apples or a few dozen eggs to "put down" in a bucket of water

glass. This took us to the carriers' stands in Mytongate near
the Market Place – a rowdy, littered channel between high old
houses that had seen better days.

Each carrier had his own stand and the street was crammed
with boxes and crates of rabbits and poultry, fruit and eggs
for sale. I wondered how the carrier remembered the owners
and destinations of much of his load – there seemed to be few
labels – and was always afraid that a package meant for
country relatives would be lost among the great piles of boxes
and bundles that filled the cart.

It wasn't just a matter of taking things into town and bringing others back; the carrier acted as messenger between
friends and relatives – no doubt many a bit of gossip, many a
rumour was transmitted along the road by this means – and
he was entrusted with a variety of commissions, especially in
the matter of buying from the town shops.

It was: "Bring me fower rowls o' wallpaper wi' a few lartle
flowers on it fer oor back bedroom."

Or: "Ah want a bottle o' that cough med'cine fre' that
chemist i' Market Place – like tha browt us last week."

Mary Fowler (1966)

BUS RIDES IN SWALEDALE

FIFTY years ago you had a choice of transport to get you
into upper Swaledale from Darlington. First you had to
get to Richmond which you could do either by train or
by one of three competing bus services. There was the United
(yellow in those days), the Express (red), or Blumer's (dark
blue). They quite literally raced each other between pick-up
points, one going by way of Gilling. Eventually they all became
part of the United network.

At Richmond you changed to Percivals' (red) or to
Scratcherd's (dark brown) to take you into the upper Dale
right up to their terminus at *The Cat Hole* Inn at Keld.
Percivals were from Gunnerside and Scratcherds from Reeth.

Percivals had a driver named Claud – well known to the
visitors though we never knew his surname. Quite imperturb-
able, he negotiated those narrow roads and even narrower

bridges with their sharp bends without seeming to hurry and on Sunday mornings he would gently swerve into farm gateways to allow a boy on the step to hurl bundled newspapers in the general direction of the distant farmhouse. Traffic was light in those days, of course, but the roads were narrower and more twisty and no small expertise was called for in handling a clumsy vehicle.

I well remember one ride behind Claud from Keld to Richmond. A fairly full bus – mostly visitors aiming to make their connections at Richmond and Darlington, and not "broken to Claud". We reached Thwaite and were about to move off when a man ran out of a house and called "Can ta wait a minit, Claud, I've a feller in?"

Claud switched off and we waited. Some of the strangers began to look at their watches and whisper together. Eventually, the man re-appeared, bag of tools in hand and square of glass under arm, business concluded, and we proceeded.

At Muker, once again Claud was about to let in his clutch when a lady came to her door and called out: "Will t'ave a cup o' tea, Claud?" Nothing loth, Claud switched off again and left us to enter the lady's house. After five or ten minutes, not only were watches being consulted but there was muttering in the ranks. The cognoscenti however were unmoved – they knew! At Reeth, Claud disappeared altogether for ten minutes. We did our best to soothe and reassure.

From Reeth to Richmond was uneventful except when we passed the "down" bus making for Reeth. The two drivers managed to draw close enough abreast to stop for a chat, permissible only because there was no traffic pressure. But our friends caught their connection(s) with time to spare – Claud had done it again!

Arthur Leng (1983)

SWALEDALE BUS

Some things and people wander passing slow,
Unchanging in their stride through weal or woe,
The Swaledale omnibus is one of these
Chuntering amongst the lanes and leafy trees,
Scarlet and yellow by dusty hedges grey
Breaking the magic of the summer's day
And breaking, breathing yet a magic still,
Climbing the sleepy hollow and the hill.

Garlic, anemone and celandine
Green swards empeopled by fat, speckled kine
Or infant piglets gam'bling in the sun,
Their future still obscure, yet Life begun,
Close by the street as sleepy, shuddering through,
The village church clock drowses half past two,
Whilst ruddy fathers 'merging from the hostelry
Slump down upon the purring red upholstery!

Stout village matrons climb aboard and then,
From out each basket blinks a startled hen;
An infant perched beside is, startled, quick,
Sucks the inevitable barley sugar stick.
Our bus awaits the postman and the mail,
Then crawling onwards lurches down the dale,
The whilst imagination skirts the brink –
– If only this droll bus could pause and think.

Back and beyond, across the sands of time,
This self-same road, this self-same Yorkshire clime;
Here marched the Roman, eagle to the sky,
Here lived the Dane when Viking hordes came by,
Here in his course the Norman trudged along
With all the gamut of HIS marching song,
'Til fat Victorians switched the pony cart,
Each in his turn, each actor to his part.

In this great scheme lost in its secrecy,
Each generation 'merging from obscurity,
Plodding through life as plodding down the dale,
Each his own story, each his separate tale,
'Til meeting here upon this summer's day.
Roman and Dane and we in English May,
Our history parading without noise or full –
– Swaledale unfolded by an omnibus!

William Hebden (1949)

ANOTHER ARTERY SEVERED

ANOTHER Dales railway line has closed down, so far as the passenger service is concerned. The Hawes–Northallerton train made its last journey a few weeks ago and another little Dales artery has been severed. On paper in a far-off London board room this doubtless appears a notable achievement, another instalment of that "rationalisation" we used to hear so much of between the wars. In Wensleydale itself there are very different views as was shown by the strength of local protects against the closure.

Already the ending of the service has proved to have many disadvantages. A local bus service, however good, cannot meet so many requirements as did the railway. Hotel and boarding house proprietors are certain to feel the effects of the closure ere long. As with the closing down of the Clapham-Tebay line, a large section of our Dales countryside is virtually cut off from the rest of the world. There have already been bitter complaints about this in the Sedbergh area. There will be others from the Wensleydale area. But they are likely to have little effect on that far-away board room.

It is odd, to say the least, that now that our railways have become a national "service", presumably run for the public benefit rather than for profit, we are getting a service that is worse in many ways than when the railways were presumably run for private gain.

Apart from the utilitarian value of the line up Wensleydale
– a value which in the opinion of many competent judges
could have been greatly increased by an alternative system
of diesel-powered trains and more attractive fares, as well
as by greater advertising – there was a scenic value in the
journey through the dale which many will miss. There was
always a quiet charm in the journey up and down the dale at
all seasons of the year, and as the railway kept to the centre
of the dale floor it commanded views which the roads on either
side miss. There was a particular fascination about a trip
which began on the rolling flat lands around Northallerton
and went deeper and deeper into the hills arriving eventually
in the wild bleak uplands of Garsdale.

Someday wiser counsels may prevail, and some of these
lost lines of Yorkshire may be restored to us with perhaps
a cheaper and more frequent service to commend them. We
shall rediscover their value both to the local communities they
were built to serve and to the holiday-makers who found them
a way of entry to the delights of our fast-vanishing countryside. Until then they must remain only a treasured memory.

"Dalesman's Diary" (1954)

10
TRAMPING THROUGH YORKSHIRE

A NEW YEAR'S DAY WALK

THE track runs from below Muker into Swaledale along Oxnop Side and over Askrigg Common into Wensleydale. It starts steeply up the hillside, a narrow road of the sort which might easily die away at a few farms. Round a hairpin bend you come to the farmhouse of Crowtrees, perched boldly and yet easefully on the slope so that its site seems the only possible one there. It gives its name to this route into the next dale.

Little humpy hillocks like fairy knolls surround Oxnop Gill on your left, and the farmhouses which stand between them, most of the cultivated meadows on their rolling surface, seem to have grown with them. Trods, the local name for paths, run in all directions from this community.

We once walked this way with a woman from one of these houses. She had been visiting in Muker, and before she took the muddy track which led to them from the road she stopped and drew out a pair of thick shoes from a hidden hole in the wall, and very sensibly changed from her visiting shoes into these.

Beyond the houses the fells merge into a rocky ledge on whose lonely heights hawks and falcons must surely have bred not so long ago. The road itself winds and twists now up a gully between rocks. Progress is slow, for you are continually looking back for the changing views of the Swaledale valley below. Presently only the far side of this remains in sight, and out of the mist which rolls on and off the fell tops you see the opening to the sombre ravine of Swinnergill, and remember how it ends at a cave with a waterfall for a door.

As you mount the last rise a spiral of smoke curls into the

sky and spreads out below, and you come to two roadmen
sitting round the fire as they eat their lunch. They ask you
the time, and their nod as you tell them shows that their own
observations on the progress of the day had been correct. A
few more steps, and all view of the valley has vanished, but
the remembrance of it is still vivid as you reach the summit
and the voices of the roadmen, singing as they prepare for
work again, waft up the gill.

Ella Pontefract (1940)

UNCHARTED COURSE

L OVELY Colsterdale! We saw it for the first time in the
red gold light of its blazing autumn trees. Coming so
suddenly from the wild moors to its peaceful farms and
calm little river, there was something unreal and impossible
about it. Even the war-time lumber camp could not dispel the
feeling that this was a place apart ... Walking up-valley, following, so our map told us, the River Burn, we were strangely
thrilled by the beauty of this newly discovered dale. We
determined to walk on to its head and then cut across the
intervening moor to Coverdale.

And so we came up the dale, until at the last farm we were
directed to turn right where a track led over the shoulder
of Masham Moor and down to Coverdale. First, crossing a
field, we encountered two rams chained together, grazing in
enforced unison. They raised their heads, nervously, stared,
and then bolted with a ghostly clanking into the mist. The
grassland ended abruptly and we found ourselves among the
heather and bracken again. Lovely colours there were among
the humble moorland plants: gold bracken, emerald moss, and
every shade from chrome to scarlet among the dying bilberry
leaves. The path cut deep into the ground, high earthy banks
shut us in so that we could follow no landmarks. There was a
stream below on the right which did not feature on our map,
and soon, as we got higher, those elusive peaks appeared again,
this time behind us. Obviously they could have no connection
with the Whernsides, which must be on our left! It was not
until much later, however, that we admitted to being "lost".

Then the track had left us, with disconcerting finality, in the middle of a peat bog.

The dampness, which for some time past had clung unobtrusively to our sweaters and hair and eyebrows, now turned to stinging rain. The mist came down in a solid wall. The grouse hurled themselves from under our feet and mockingly ordered us to "Go-back!" Lost! We sat among the peat-hags and ate scones and cheese. We tried to work out compass bearings, we tried to guess the time, and having decided, all things considered, that wherever we might be, the course was *West*, we started off. It was a case of "through everything" – heather and grass and peat – until we should strike a path or watercourse.

Before long our legs were scratched and bleeding; sodden boots squelched water through the lace-holes at every step. Still we kept on, till the mist shifted and we saw a stream ahead. Assuredly a tributary of the Cover! Tripping and stumbling through the knee-high heather, falling into hidden streamlets, at last we found a path. Our spirits rose at every step on the firm ground as we marched down the trackway. But then, oh, horror! there appeared a small cairn of stones *which we had seen before*. We looked at one another, incredulous in chagrin and anxiety. "It's not possible. We *can't* have walked in a circle." But there, convincing evidence, were our own boot marks imprinted on the track, and coming *the same way*. In grim silence we carved a *third* pattern of nail prints as we tramped back again to the same peat bog.

Another compass bearing sent us off again through the soaking heather, walking desperately against time with four hours of daylight left. Crossing a stream we stopped for a drink of its peat-stained water (looking for all the world like mild ale). Then on again until we found the first of three tall boundary stones, inscribed with the names of by-gone landowners. A cheering sight – it hinted, at least, of civilisation.

Presently through the clearing rain, we picked out a fence on the skyline. Aiming straight for it in the hope of finding a path, we were horribly "bogged". After that we paid more respect to the warning of smooth green patches. Short cuts are apt to be the longest, particularly on Yorkshire moors. Beyond the wire fence we came to a disused slate quarry, and still there was no sign of road or trackway. We had hoped to strike the Arkleside path, but here things seemed quite unfamiliar. Picking a route downhill we aimed for distant farm buildings – Swineside as we later discovered – and ran down the steep slope of fields, rucksacks bumping our backs, the soft brown featheriness of seeding grasses caressing our bleeding shins. We felt ridiculously happy, such was the relief of being off the moor, of knowing what river that was, of seeing houses and a road.

J.E. Hemingway (1944)

COASTWISE TEMPTATIONS

"**L**OOK," I said, "If we ignore that path and cut down that valley – that one right ahead – we'll reach the shore and then we can paddle back to Robin Hood's Bay." The others said it was a good idea at the time although they denied it later.

The valley, you see, played me false. It was not a valley at all. It was a ravine with banks of shale. It was shaped like a V and a stream ran at the bottom through a tight mass of undergrowth. The others scrambled along the shaly banks, muttering unkindly. I walked along the shaly stream bed, thinking that I was getting my paddle anyway, that my toes would dry out, and that sticks and stones might break my bones but words would never hurt me.

As the valley deepened and steepened a dread suspicion crossed my mind which was amply confirmed when Harry, once again in the lead, shouted "Back, back" like Napoleon in Moscow. That wretched valley ended not on the shore but above it – 100 feet up a sheer cliff. The stream, having shared our company, took its leave and plunged over the top, gurgling and splashing in high glee.

We had no intention of imitating it. Instead we climbed the northern bank of the ravine, scrambling up on all fours. Nor were our tribulations to end. "The thing to remember," said Derek severely, "is that when you find a good path, stick to it." At the time we were standing in a lushly overgrown bog in the middle of a field which had a bull in it.

Harry contented himself with asking for the return of

the map.

I squelched in the water swilling about between my toes and hoped that the gambolling Whizz would not incite or otherwise inflame the bull. We re-joined the path by devious means and there encountered two girls with trim legs ending incongruously in hob nailed boots. They told us they had walked from the Youth Hostel at Scarborough. The hostel, they added righteously, had a specific warning about the coast-wise temptations north of Ravenscar.

"Never mind," said the prettier one, charmingly, "You've done jolly well for middle-aged men."

Malcolm Barker (1966)

INGLEBOROUGH WAY

FROM Trow Gill it is a very easy stroll to Ingleborough top and in spite of recent rains the going was quite good. I paused when I came to Gaping Gill, for I can never resist the temptation to lie down on the edge and peer into its depths, then by bearing a little to the left I managed to keep a reasonably dry course. As I reached the stony slope just below the first cairn, and I looked back over the Allotment and Sulber Moss, the moorland colours softened into velvet tones of olive, varied greens and brown.

Pen-y-ghent, now somewhat dwarfed, still looked imposing, as it always must from the west, and then I gained the ridge and looked westward beyond Ingleton and the Greta. The countryside lay under a huge fog bank, not white or grey, not swirling or drifting, but uniform, dark puce-coloured, motionless and featureless, just an impenetrable blank in the landscape. But from its farthest depth there rose a group of mountain tops, clear slate-blue against the sky, Great Gable, Great End, Bowfell, Scafell Pike, Scafell and the Crinkles. A little further to the south, the point of Black Combe showed rather faintly in the distance, and fifteen degrees to northward of the main group, a small cluster which seemed unmistakably to include Helvellyn and the sharp ridge of Catchedicam. Southward the fog shut out everything beyond a few miles' range, but where I stood the sun was really powerful and until I reached the cairn on Ingleborough top there was scarcely enough wind to blow out a candle flame.

Northward the air was clear. The mass of Whernside shut out the panorama of peaks further north, but beyond Great Coum the lovely Howgills looked inviting as ever. To the west, the mist seemed to be creeping slowly higher and nearer. The Scafell group grew smaller but they still reared their heads above it. As I watched, a white point of cloud appeared in the hollow of Great End, rising perhaps over Angle Tarn, a white plume flew from Great Gable and I thought of that June day of sunshine and fast moving shadows, when I had sat on the topmost point of Honister Crag and watched white clouds roll over Gable, as a mist rolls slowly landward across a windless sea. That day, in spite of the fresh breeze, a bank of pure white cloud lay motionless on Pillar, and though shining tongues of cloud crept like live things down the gulleys on the northern face, the summit never cleared. That is a thing I have never seen in the Pennines, stationary banks of white cloud on the hilltops on a day of brilliant sunshine. I have seen the grey mist swirling down the hillside and heavy wet, grey clouds lying for days on the tops but never those still white banks of fleece.

As I made my way northward towards the col and Simon Fell, the broad shadow of Ingleborough lay across the hollow to my left. Below, towards Black Shiver Moss, the moor was a soft brown, almost cinnamon, but the curving hillside reaching up to the col was literally blue, believe it or not, a soft misty blue like nigella in bloom. A trick of the sunlight and a slight mistiness in the air no doubt, but blue it was. Before I reached the summit of Park Fell, the mist had crept up all round. Pen-y-ghent had completely disappeared. Whernside was scarcely visible and mist lay even on the slope of Simon Fell behind me. Only Ingleborough top stood proudly in the sunshine, the wide table-land and the magnificent western terraces. Druidical lusts indeed! It looked more like the mountain of the blest.

Francis Edge (1949)

A WHIT WALK

IN the early days of the century the annual Sunday School scholars' walk was a feature of every West Riding village at Whitsuntide. At one o'clock the grand procession began. First came the farm wagon, covered with bunting and ribbon, carrying the infants; the horse decorated with plaited tail, rosettes and bells, and the farmer's man, almost unrecognisable, in his billy cock and polished leggings.

A second wagon contained John William and the harmonium. This was a matter of annual shame. Unlike the church, we could not afford a brass band. The harmonium had one castor missing, and, although the foot was propped with two hymn books and roped tightly to the shafts, it slithered about alarmingly and showed a disconcerting propensity to rock dangerously at corners or when the loud pedal was depressed. The prim young lady who played it so melodiously on Sundays refused to occupy the stool, and John William, who agonised the whole village with some of his notes, had to be substituted.

We were not the only Sunday School walking and the choirmaster always urged: "Tha mun play varry softly, John William, if awther t'Wesleyans or t'Rehoboth is onywheer near."

The classes followed in order of age, males and females being severely separated. The blare of the church's brass band would come from the other end of the village and send a jealous and subconscious flash across the face of the superintendent, standing among the children in the first cart.

The walking tended to become a little boring and there were grossly unfair inconsistencies. If I whispered to my friend: "They say Lancashire hev lost four wickets in t'first hour this morning," my mother would sneak behind me at the next stopping place and, prodding me with her umbrella, threaten, "If tha talks ageean I shall tell thi father when I get home."

But from the adult ladies' class came a constant murmur of: "Aye, I allus say Whitsuntide is a bad time for chickenpox, Mrs. Jagger's youngest hes it. When I looked in this morning t'poor bairn was so covered wi' spots yo' couldn't hev put a pin dahn on her."

Nevertheless there would be compensations. There would be that pretty lass from the Methodists to smile at as we passed their procession, and, by gosh! she'd smile back at me.

There would be dancing in the Methodists' field at night, and there was a hole in the wall behind the mistal where I could sneak in. Even mother's cold douche of: "Tha ought to be ashamed o' thisen, winking at that fast hussy from t'Methodists. I'll let thy father knaw abaht thee when I get home toneet, lad," could not stay my resolve.

Reluctantly, as evening fell, I was last to leave the field, wandering slowly to where Nemesis waited. As I opened the door mother snapped with relish: "Aye, come in if tha dare. I've never felt so ashamed in all my life. I've telled thi father all abaht how tha's disgraced us. What does tha think abaht him, George?"

I turned to my father. There seemed little anger and much pleasure in his countenance. "Tha hears what thi mother says," he said, "Nay, I'm fair capped with thee, lad," and, without a pause, continued: "Has tha heard that Yorkshire's won bi aboot an innings? By gum, lad, if they're doing as weel next year and, same as thi mother says, tha misbehaves thisen at t'Sunday Schooil walk, tha'll hev to come wi' me to t'match at Old Trafford."

Harry East (1965)

11
FOOD
FOR THOUGHT

YORKSHIRE PUDDINGS

DAD always wanted roast beef and Yorkshire Pudding on Sundays, except at Christmas when a bird of some sort of another was our repast. We girls were more than happy with this decision and would hover around mum, no doubt getting under her feet, anxious in case not enough of the precious pale creamy yellow liquid was mixed.

We took it in turns to beat up the pudding mixture, and small hands had to be careful to hold on to the large white bowl lest the precious contents be spilled. No electric blenders for us, just a large table fork and a lot of patience as we slowly added the flour to the egg, milk and water.

The fire oven, by now well and truly stoked up, would cause spitting and popping noises to emit from within as the large joint of beef gave up some of its juices and mingled with the beef dripping. Potatoes grown in the garden at the back of the house, peeled and prepared before church going, would soon be joining the meat where they would take on lovely shades of gold to brown. Vegetables, also home grown, would vary with the seasons.

Soon the moment we had been waiting for arrived. Clutching a good thick cloth the oven would be opened by mum, and into it placed four seven-inch round sandwich tins, each bearing a small mound of beef dripping. The tins would be left in the oven until the fat melted and smoked slightly blue, not burnt mind you, just extremely hot.

Meanwhile the pudding mixture received its final beating. Mum insisted it was important to get as much air as possible into the plain flour mixture. Quick as a flash, the tins would be out of the oven, half the mixture shared equally between the four tins, and back into the oven before losing any of their precious heat.

By this time the joint was resting on its dish prior to carving, the rich brown gravy brought to boiling point and four warmed dinner plates laid out to receive their ambrosial offerings. Hair combed and hands washed, Marjorie and I would sit up at the table like two young greyhounds waiting for the "off".

At last, the first course was set in front of us, a large, light as air, slightly crisp at the edges, true Yorkshire Pudding and a stream of delicious gravy poured into the centre. All served, we would contentedly munch our way through this long awaited delight. No need to scold us for talking at the table; we were too busy eating.

This, of course, is the traditional way to eat Yorkshire Pudding, a separate course followed by the beef and vegetables, but mum, with love and understanding of our requests for more, would repeat the process of the pudding baking with the other half of the mixture, timing them to be eaten with our main course. Mm! Delicious!

Audrey Ely-Booth (1984)

OATCAKE

THE thin oatcake was made from a mixture of oatmeal, salt, often a little yeast, and water. It was mixed thinly with the hand in a small kneading tub or bowl called a 'nakit', and left to stand for a night. The bowl was seldom washed, but was scraped round with a knife, leaving some of the mixture on the sides to ferment. In some districts, notably Westmorland, this was the only raising agent used.

The cakes were cooked on a backstone, a stone or iron slab built over a small, closed-in fire. The surviving backstones are practically all iron, but place names, such as Backstone Beck near Masham, Backstone Gill in Nidderdale and Backstone Edge on Askrigg Moor, show that stone slabs were quarried here, and must have been used extensively.

In country districts a farmhouse possessing a backstone often served the neighbourhood. Older people in Barden in

Wharfedale still tell how the farmers' wives made their own mixture, and took it on certain days of the week to be cooked on the backstone at Gamsworth.

This type of oatcake was also made in bakeries and the art was passed down from one generation to another. It was delivered in many districts round the towns. Many West Riding people remember the oatcake man resting his large deep basket on the doorstep while he turned back the white covering cloths and counted out the thin cakes; and how a few of the cakes were spread with butter, and sometimes treacle as well, and rolled up and eaten while still soft. The people in the neighbourhood of Huddersfield were fond of 'browis', which was oatcake soaked in broth or gravy.

Ella Pontefract (1943)

SINFUL EXTRAVAGANCE

W E went to [a Nidderdale] farm for tea – everything homemade, of course, including the beef which was served warm with gravy in which, with a feeling of sinful extravagance, I was invited by example to dip the generously buttered bread!

That beef! Odes have been written on much less worthy themes! The gods on Olympus would have wolfed it gratefully. I have dined, at the expense of various employers, in many expensive hotels in many capitals, but never tasted such meat since! It remains an undying memory of heavenly succulence and ineffable tenderness to which I simply can't do justice.

James R. Gregson (1968)

COTTAGE TEAS

W HAT I really missed, without knowing how much until I met it again, was the friendly sign on wayside farm or cottage that says simply "TEAS". That sign, as frequent in the North as it is rare in Midland, East Anglian or many Southern counties, indicates something more than

refreshment. At best, it means "Come in, sit thee down and mak' thiself at home."

The meaning of "tea" itself is, of course, as different in the North as Wensleydale is from mousetrap cheese. If you do find a TEA sign in other parts you may count yourself lucky to get three or four limp pieces of bread, a smear of synthetic jam and a couple of bought cakes in crinkly paper. There's certainly no hope of a "high" tea, except perhaps in the charge.

But in the Pennine country people simply would not go in for this sort of tea – not twice. Every cottager and farmer's wife knows this. So when you ask for tea, they adopt a sort of defensive gambit: "Well, I've nothing much for tea today, really," they say, and then, doubtfully, "but come in."

Do not worry; within five minutes you will be sitting down at a table entirely covered with curd tarts, girdle cakes, freshly-baked currant teacake, ginger bread, sweet loaf, home-made damson jam or lemon cheese, supported by several plates of wholemeal biscuits and crisp bread and butter.

If you are lucky there may be a plate of hot apple tart or onion scones as well. Yet to someone who has been out on the fells all day or walked half the length of the dale, these are only frills. The first question *he* expects when he asks for tea is: "Will you have one egg with your ham or two?"

Alan Walbank (1956)

12
A YORKSHIRE MISCELLANY

MILL LIFE

I LEFT school in 1908 at the age of fourteen and got work in a mill as a spinner. In the ordinary way I should have started work as a half-timer at twelve but because of a recurrent illness I had missed a lot of schooling, so I was allowed to go until the full school-leaving age. This suited me because I liked school but, with five children in the family, even the small wages of a half-timer were helpful.

We lived in the country and the mills were a long way from

home. I began work at a mill about two-and-a-half miles away and five of us from the same village accompanied each other to and from work. The memory of those early morning walks, especially in summer, with distant woods in view and horses and cows peacefully grazing in dew-wet pastures for miles around, brings to mind the words of a dales shepherd whom Halliwell Sutcliffe quoted in his book *The Striding Dales* "... Every morning, as if you watched creation all afresh."

I remember too those clear, cold winter mornings when the leafless hedgerows sparkled with frosty diamonds in the dawn-light. Somehow, the return journeys never seemed to have the same magic.

The only real hardships from the weather were the mornings when it was snowing or raining heavily and we were "sodden to t'skin" literally. Sometimes our shawls and top-coats were not quite dry as we put them on again to leave work, but getting wet on the return journey we could change into dry clothing at home and our wet garments were spread out on the clothes-horse near the fire.

In the very dark weather we made lanterns consisting of lighted carriage candles stuck inside glass jam jars; they were carried by means of wire instead of string. The "townies" teased us at work about our "lanterns".

The working hours were six-to-six during the week, and from six to twelve-thirty on Saturdays. I set off from home at 5 a.m. and mother got up about an hour earlier to light the fire on which to boil the kettle; we had neither gas nor electricity. She always prepared a good breakfast and "put my jock up" (food for the day) before I left. In later years I realised what long "working hours" our mother had. Life seemed to have been "all bed and work" at our house, but we were happy and contented.

The wages in the spinning department were 4s. a week but later (after a brief strike!) they were increased to 4s. 6d. My work-mates told me I was lucky because, being exceptionally tall (growin' past mi strength!) I was given the job of roving-putter-in which added another sixpence to my wages!

Father started work in a mill at the age of eight; he was so small that he was provided with a buffet on which to stand to enable him to do his work. He was "sacked" almost every day for falling asleep but he always turned up again next day. The first time he did so the overlooker said: "I thowt I'd sacked thi," to which my father replied: "Yes, sir, but that was yesterday."

Amy Jackson (1970)

SATURDAY NIGHTS

SATURDAY, after tea, in the 1950s, was always the same – taking out the black silk faced dinner jacket, and black silk-striped trousers from the wardrobe, brushing the fabric to remove any loose hairs, or mud splashes from the trousers, then pressing them up to create some immaculate creases.

After I had had a bath, I donned a white shirt and black bow tie, the newly-pressed dinner jacket and trousers, also polished black shoes. I was ready to play four hours of dancing at one of the frequent Saturday night hops in Linton Village Hall.

What wonderful times we had, being a star attraction in the Dales. We of the Craven Players were good pals and enjoyed our playing. Maybe we were not musicians with the impact of those bigger bands that graced the Town Hall, Clifford Hall or "t'Welfare" in Skipton during that period, but we enjoyed playing our style of music. The many people who followed us from village hall to village hall thought we were the tops.

These dances took place all year round, moving from village to village. Every New Year's Eve saw us in Grassington Town Hall. We were also there on Easter Monday and August Bank Holiday Monday. Burnsall Sports were followed by a dance. The Kilnsey Show dance was sometimes held in a marquee or in the village hall, with the band sitting on the billiards table. Kettlewell dances were from 10p.m. until 2a.m. and often a collection was taken so that we might play for another hour (the late start was because a whist drive took place first).

We once saw the dawn break after a dance at Kettlewell. We had been taken to Kettlewell in an old Rolls Royce taxi, the driver saying he had to take a fare to Leeds when he got back to Skipton, but that he would return to Kettlewell. The dance was a huge success, with dancers coming from miles away in vans and Landrovers. At 2a.m., the dance was still very lively and the MC asked if we would play for another hour if they took a collection for us. We said we would play until the taxi came. Little did we know what lay ahead.

By three o'clock, we were pretty well shattered. But still there was no sign of the taxi, and the dancers were making their way home. So we packed up and trundled all our instruments and tackle down to the bridge to wait our transport. Shortly after 4a.m. we spotted a twinkling light way down the road, and waited seemingly ages for the car to arrive. As it did, we could see the dawn breaking over the hills to the east.

Fastened to the front of the old Rolls was a paraffin storm light and another painted red was at the rear. The driver explained that after he had dropped his fare in Leeds, all his electrical circuits had fused or burnt out, so he had no lights, nor horn. He managed to join some wire together to get the engine started and picked up the storm lamps at some roadworks and quietly made his way to Kettlewell.

Bill Miles (1987)

WHEN I WAS NOBBUT A LAD

ONCE upon a time – it was in that mixed era when Victorians and Edwardians overlapped; when old values and customs died hard and new ones fought for supremacy; well, I was nobbut a lad, living in Percy Street in Neepsend, Sheffield.

Yes, I can imagine some folk saying: "What! *that* mucky 'ole?"... But as I've said I was a lad, and it seemed "all reight to me."

It was a time when the School Board Man was as much the parents' bogey as the children's. When the pawnbroker was everybody's Uncle, and fish and chips tasted better out of the paper than off a plate.

I remember, at that time, taking a babby's pram or a home-made barrow to fetch "Three pennorth o' coil" from the coal yard in the street.

There was a good deal of poverty in those days. Fires, more often than not, were banked-up with slack to "mak' it last longer". I can see the thick yellow smoke puffing out of the

grate and curling round the bars before finding its way up
the chimney.

But on baking days, the fires glowed warmly; on the hearths
would be earthenware panchions filled with dough breathing
gently like soft white bellies... and when we came home from
school there'd be lovely hungry smells of newly baked bread.

Some days in the week the cupboards in Percy Street would
be practically bare... Still, there'd always be brimstone and
treacle, which was a handy cure for all our childish ailments.
When I had a cold my mother rubbed my chest with tallow...

Taking the mester's dinner was a job I didn't mind doing.
Whenever I got the chance, I'd stop to watch the men wrestling
with the white-hot metal, as it came out of the furnaces. By
the time I'd delivered the dinner, they always complained it
was "stone cowd" and "the' wa' moor gravy in t' 'andkerchief
than in t' basin."

The three pubs in Percy Street were referred to as "boozers",
and the "off-licence" as the "beer-off". I remember the pubs,
not for the drunks on Saturday nights, but for the horses
in the shafts of the brewers' drays. How well, strong, cared
for they looked. Sometimes their manes were plaited with
coloured horse ribbons and you could see your face in the
brass on the shining harness.

Although there wasn't much drinking in our house, I loathed
being sent to fetch beer from the "beer-off". But this only
happened when cump'ny came.

Once I remember being sent out to fetch "a quart". As I
was bringing it back I saw my Sunday School teacher coming
towards me. Hoping she hadn't "twigged" I pushed the bottle
up my jersey... I'd always been taught to "mind mi manners"
and as she passed I withdrew the hand supporting it, to raise
my cap. There was a deafening crash as the bottle reached
the pavement and the frothy liquid swirled round my feet.

William Taylor (1959)

DALESFOLK

YOU must weather the Dalesfolk to know them – not just idle among them as a "towrist" on a summer day. And let me tell you the dalesfolk are not impressed by "them towrists" who are mostly afraid of cows. If you can plunge through inky lanes on dense black nights, with an east wind blizzard facing you, and sheets of rain or slanting snow in your face, a lantern in your own hand – then you get to know the Dale and become "one of us". In a Burberry and a sou-wester you can enjoy it. Once, I went out in a sou-wester in Ripon. I hadn't the courage to do it again.

Grand, indomitable, independent, and individual, are the Dalesfolk. One reads in foolish London publications that outstanding characters are things of the past, and that humanity has become uniform. To look at the monotonous appearance of towns-people would seem to bear that out, but in the Dale they are just as individual as ever. One has only to board the bus in Ripon market place, and travel up to Hawes, to prove this. The last time I enjoyed that journey, one could tell by the hats in the bus what sort of personalities were underneath them. You couldn't do that in Harrogate.

When we acquired our Wensleydale cottage, we arrived there on a Tuesday, in a wet August. Forgetting that Wednesday would be early closing day, after a busy morning we went down to Hawes to buy food. We found all the shops shut except the green-grocer's. And he might sell only what was perishable. We said we wanted cheese. He replied that we might have carrots. I observed that carrots were no more perishable than cheese. "Ah knoa yon," said an old dalesman, witheringly. "Bit t'law says they is, so of coorse they is." His wife was in the shop, and seeing our quandary, said to her husband "Ye might sell 'em a lile bit o' cheese." The old man, with a cheery smile, went to the door of his shop, looked up and down the street, and said "Nay, nay, if I sell her a bit I'll see as she has a pretty middlin' big piece."

Florence Bone (1939)

A FROG WITH NOWHERE TO GO

IF you are unhappy about the level of your water rates, spare a thought for the hair-raising experiences of a Yorkshire frog, caught up in a situation over which he had no control. Living as we do on the borders of Lancashire and Yorkshire, just opposite Top Withens, the supposed prototype of Wuthering Heights, pure fresh water has always been one of our delights. None of your fluoride, or even chlorine here! But it must be confessed that there are several disadvantages.

The origin of the spring which delivers to us an unending supply of water, even during the most dire days of drought elsewhere, is unknown, though we suspect that it is either under or just across the road – at any rate not far from the main collecting point. Support for this view is given by the fact that is is extremely acid – presumably, the water experts say, because it travels a short distance over peat, and does not come into contact with limestone at all.

There are other hazards too. Since the pump which delivers the water to the house has to be housed in the garage outside to avoid the airlocks which occur if it is inside, there is the constant threat of freezing up in the severe winters we have way up on the Pennines; trying to work out if the sudden stoppage of water is due to a breakdown of the supply en route from the collecting tank, to the brushes having been worn out or to the heavily lagged piping having been defeated by the level of frost, is not a welcome exercise when the winds are blowing so hard and bitter that they are turning the evergreens brown.

The grand climax came the other day. After installing a brand new tank and larger polythene pipes one inch in diameter to replace lead ones which were 80 years old, we thought that one, at least, of the hazards would be behind us. But suddenly the supply came to a halt, and this on a bright autumn day when no frost problems could be to blame. Graham, our plumber, was for once stumped. The supply *ought* to be there; there was nothing to stop it, and any debris from the base of the collecting tank would have been able to escape easily from the wider pipes which had been installed.

There was nothing for it but to start digging again to see

where the water was coming to a stop. The solution was not long in coming. At the stopcock which governed the diversion of the supply to two smaller pipes the culprit was found. It was a frog.

Graham was not totally surprised, since he had discovered its mate sitting on the bottom of the collecting point right at the beginning of the investigation. It was, amazingly enough, still alive, and when placed by the stream it soon disappeared, to live again in its own habitat. Imagine the terror which it must have experienced; caught by the swirl of water leaving the tank (even though the outlet is a few inches from the bottom) it must have been pushed, willy nilly, for some 150 yards along a pipe which would accommodate it without much difficulty.

We are delighted, of course, to have our water supply with us once again. It's no joke carrying all your water – how much we use – and having to think twice about how you brush your teeth. But at least we were better off than the frog. Not better off though, then the people who unthinkingly draw water whenever they wish, who do not have to listen to make sure that the tank is filling up, and who have the luxury of complaining every year, or more often, about how expensive the water supply has become. If you are one of these, whenever you are inclined to grumble, just think of the frog. He would probably prefer the public water supply, but he is not allowed to get anywhere near it. There just isn't any justice in life.

Frank Pedley (1986)